CREWE TO WIGAN

including
Over & Wharton

Adrian Hartless

Series editor Vic Mitchell

MP Middleton Press

Front cover: Preserved Coronation Pacific no. 46233 Duchess of Sutherland *accelerates away from Crewe at Coppenhall Moss on 9th September 2013 with the '75th Anniversary Special'. The train commemorated the introduction to service of the Coronations in 1938; the class worked the heaviest Anglo Scottish services on the West Coast route for some 25 years. Many thought them the finest of all British steam locos, combining power, speed and gracefulness. No. 46233 was initially saved from scrap by the Billy Butlin organisation, which displayed it at a holiday camp in Ayrshire from 1964 until 1970. It was then sold to the Bressingham Steam Museum in Norfolk, where it was occasionally steamed on a short length of track. In late 1995 it changed hands again, moving to Butterley, Derbyshire, under the ownership of the Princess Royal Class Locomotive Trust. It was returned to main line condition with the assistance of the Heritage Lottery Fund and, in 2017, was still a main line performer. The '75th Anniversary Special' took it from Crewe to Perth, a regular turn for this class in steam days, returning the following day. (J.Whitehouse)*

Back cover: Railway Clearing House map for 1947.

ACKNOWLEDGEMENTS

This book is dedicated to the memory of my Mother, who took me on a trainspotters' special train from Tamworth to Crewe Works (where no. 46220 *Coronation* was receiving its final overhaul) as an 11th birthday present, and also to Jill for her greatly valued encouragement. Additionally, I am very grateful for the assistance received from many of those mentioned in the credits, also from A.J.Castledine, G.Croughton, G.Gartside, C.M.Howard and N.Langridge.

Published November 2017

ISBN 978 1 910356 12 8

© *Middleton Press, 2017*

Production Editor Deborah Esher
Design Cassandra Morgan
Cover design Matthew Esher

Published by
   Middleton Press
   Easebourne Lane
   Midhurst
   West Sussex
   GU29 9AZ
Tel: 01730 813169
Email: info@middletonpress.co.uk
www.middletonpress.co.uk

Printed and bound by CPI Group (UK) Ltd, Croydon, CR0 4YY

INDEX

46	Acton Bridge	62	Moore
98	Bamfurlong	29	Over & Wharton
1	Crewe	57	Preston Brook
94	Golborne South	73	Warrington Bank Quay
35	Hartford	114	Wigan North Western
22	Minshull Vernon	25	Winsford

GEOGRAPHICAL SETTING

The route from Crewe is initially north westward down the Weaver Valley with a ruling gradient of 1 in 300. This is a sedimentary basin mainly given over to farming, although the UK's only major natural salt deposits are encountered around Winsford. After Weaver Junction, the line's basic trajectory is northwards. It cuts through a low ridge with a short tunnel south of Preston Brook, and then descends to cross the River Mersey on its approach to Warrington. This is punctuated by the crossing of the Manchester Ship Canal, which requires gradients in each direction of 1 in 135. Historically, the Mersey marked the boundary between Cheshire and Lancashire, but since 1974 Warrington has been relocated to the ceremonial county of Cheshire.

Beyond Warrington, the line climbs away from the Mersey valley at close to sea level, with a maximum gradient of 1 in 132, and reaches a low summit of about 150ft above sea level north of Golborne. Just before Wigan North Western station it crosses the River Douglas, which drains into the Ribble estuary. From around Golborne to Wigan the geology is carboniferous, and this area was the centre of the coal mining industry in the north west of England. Wigan, once one of the great manufacturing towns of Lancashire, has since 1974 been a district of Greater Manchester.

This part of the West Coast Main Line is now covered at such high speed that this album is essential for the enjoyment of it at your own pace. Past traffic and stations are illustrated in detail, along with the many fascinating bridges, viaducts and factories.

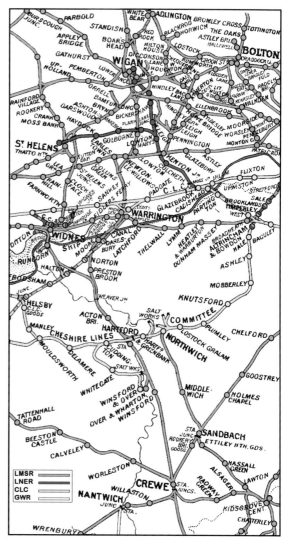

I. Railway Clearing House map for 1947.

HISTORICAL BACKGROUND

The Grand Junction Railway, Britain's first trunk railway line, opened on 4th July 1837 between Birmingham and Warrington, and was the first to serve Crewe. At Warrington, it linked up with the Warrington & Newton Railway, which opened on 25th July 1831. This, in turn, joined the Liverpool & Manchester Railway of 1830, and so it became possible to travel between Birmingham and Liverpool and Manchester by train. In 1838, the London & Birmingham Railway was completed, and thus the capital and the north west became connected by this new form of transport.

The opening day of the Grand Junction was, unusually, not marked by celebrations along its route. King William IV had died on 20th June 1837, and his funeral was not held until 8th July, so there was a mood of national mourning and understandable restraint.

Wigan was also connected to the Liverpool & Manchester, from 3rd September 1832, and this line pushed northwards to Preston from 31th October 1838, thence to Lancaster in 1840 and Carlisle in 1846. By then all the railways mentioned above had combined to form the London & North Western Railway.

In 1848, the Caledonian Railway opened from Edinburgh and Glasgow to Carlisle, completing the first Anglo-Scottish railway. The last link in the West Coast Main Line was opened between Winwick and Golborne Junctions on 1st August 1864, which avoided the Liverpool & Manchester Railway and the associated junctions and sharp curves at Earlestown and Parkside.

The LNWR became a major constituent of the London Midland & Scottish Railway on 1st January 1923, and the WCML southwards from Carlisle passed to the London Midland Region of British Railways on 1st January 1948.

Steam trains could be seen between Crewe and Wigan almost up to their elimination from the national network in August 1968. Diesels took over the express passenger services from the late 1950s, but they were replaced by electric traction as shown below. Virgin Trains has provided the West Coast Main Line services, since the train operating companies were largely returned to private ownership in 1997.

The Over & Wharton Branch has its brief history detailed in captions VII and 29 to 32.

Electrification

The inauguration of electric train services on the LMR on the 25kV AC overhead system radiated from Crewe, effective from the following dates:

Crewe – Manchester Piccadilly	12/09/1960
Crewe – Liverpool Lime Street via Weaver Jct	01/01/1962
Crewe – Stafford	07/01/1963
Stafford – London Euston (in stages)	06/11/1965
Weaver Junction – Preston	23/07/1973

II. Gradient profile

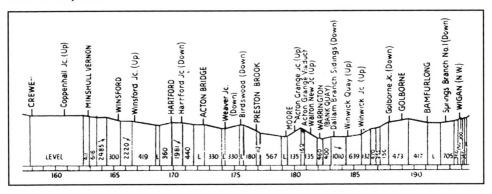

PASSENGER SERVICES

The table below indicates the number of down trains (northwards) in sample years. Initially, the calling patterns were irregular. The figures in brackets show the number of trains listed which called at most of the intermediate stations. Those running on less than five days per week are not shown; neither are those not stopping at Crewe, or not starting there.

	Weekdays	**Sundays**
1885	16 (4)	7 (3)
1910	14 (7)	7 (2)
1925	10 (1)	4 (1)
1938	13 (1)	6 (2)
1947	11 (1)	8 (1)
1963	15 (5)	9 (1)
1985	12	9

To travel between intermediate stations after about 1915 involved changing trains at Warrington, usually. The same applied until about 1890. The final figures include the many sleeper services over the route. Their times were inconvenient for most local passengers.

Sec. & Gen. Manager, Capt. Mark Huish. **GRAND JUNCTION** Treasurer, Thos. Goalen.

Distances.	Down Trains. STATIONS.	8 30 p.m. Mixed. Lon. Mail.	6 a.m. 1st & 2nd class	6 15 a.m. Mixed Mail	9 a.m. 1st class mixed	10 a.m. Lon. Mail	7 a.m. 3rd class. slow.	11 a.m. 1st class mixed	1 p.m. 1st & 2nd class	Sunday Trains. Stop at 1st cls. stas. only. 8 30 p.m mix. mail	7½ a.m. mix. & 3rd clss.	11¼ a.m. mix. Mail.	10 a.m. Mail mixed	Fares frm Birming: By 2 15 p.m.	First Class.	Second Class.	Third Class.
Mls.	**London, Euston Sq.**	8 30	..	6 15	9 0	10 0	7 0	11 0	1 0	8 30	..	..	10 0				
	Birmingham..........	**1** 10	**6**	**11¼**	**1½**	**2¼**	**3½**	**4¼**	**6**	**1** 10	**7½**	**11¼**	**2¼**	s. d.	s. d.	s. d.	s. d.
3¼	Perry Bar	..	6 9	..	..	..	3 41	..	6 9	..	..	..	..	....	0 9	0 6	0 4
6¾	Newton Road	..	6 19	..	..	..	3 53	..	6 19	..	..	..	..	....	1 6	1 0	0 7
9½	**Walsall**	..	6 29	11 37	1 54	..	4 4	4 39	6 29	..	7 49	11 37	..	....	2 0	1 6	0 10
12	Willenhall........	..	6 38	..	..	..	4 14	..	6 38	..	..	..	..	....	2 6	1 6	1 0
14¼	**Wolverhampton**	1 45	6 47	11 52	2 9	2 50	4 24	4 52	6 47	1 45	8 5	11 52	2 50	3 6	3 0	2 0	1 3
20	Four Ashes	..	7 2	..	..	..	4 43	..	7 2	..	..	..	..	....	5 0	3 6	1 8
21½	Spread Eagle	..	7 10	..	..	..	4 51	..	7 10	..	..	..	..	....	5 0	3 6	1 10
24	Penkridge........	..	7 19	..	..	..	5 0	5 16	7 19	..	..	..	..	....	5 6	4 0	2 0
29¼	**Stafford**........	2 17	7 32	12 17	2 41	3 22	5 17	5 31	7 31	2 17	8 30	12 17	3 22	7 0	6 0	5 0	2 6
35	Norton Bridge........	..	7 51	..	2 59	..	5 55	..	7 50	..	..	..	..	....	7 6	6 6	2 11
43¼	**Whitmore**	2 55	8 16	12 55	3 24	4 0	6 32	6 9	8 13	2 55	9 8	12 55	4 0	11 6	10 6	8 0	3 3
46	Madeley........	..	8 27	..	..	..	6 45	..	8 23	..	..	..	..	....	11 0	8 6	3 10
51½	Basford........	..	8 41	..	..	..	7 31	..	8 36	..	..	..	..	....	12 6	9 6	4 4
54	**Crewe**	3 19	8 48	1 19	3 49	4 24	7 39	6 34	8 43	3 19	9 32	1 19	4 24	14 6	13 0	10 6	4 6
53¾	Minshull Vernon	..	9 3	..	..	..	8 1	..	8 56	..	..	..	..	....	14 0	11 0	4 11
61¼	Winsford	..	9 12	..	4 9	..	8 10	..	9 4	..	..	..	..	....	14 6	11 6	5 2
65¾	**Hartford**........	3 44	9 24	1 44	4 21	4 49	8 24	7 2	9 15	3 44	9 57	1 44	4 49	17 6	16 0	12 6	5 6
68¼	Acton........	..	9 33	..	..	..	8 35	..	9 24	..	..	..	..	....	16 6	12 6	5 9
72½	Preston Brook........	..	9 46	2 0	..	..	8 49	..	9 36	..	..	2 0	..	....	17 0	13 6	6 1
75	Moore	..	9 55	..	..	..	8 58	..	9 45	..	..	..	..	....	18 0	14 0	6 3
78	**Warrington**	4 12	10 4	2 16	4 48	5 17	9 16	7 30	9 54	4 12	10 25	2 16	5 17	21 0	19 0	14 6	6 6
82¾	Newton Junction	4 28	10 19	..	..	..	9 33	..	10 8	..	..	..	..	..	21 0	15 6	6 11
97	**Liverpool**........	5 10	11 15	3 15	5 45	6 15	10 30	8 30	11 0	5 10	1 10	3 15	6 15	26 0	23 0	18 0	8 2
75	**Chester**........	4 6	10 16	2 42	..	5 19	..	8 21	..	4 0	..	..	5 19	20 0	18 0	14 0	6 3
105¾	**Preston**........	5 24	1 45	3 40	..	6 40	..	..	..	5 4	..	..	6 40	..	..	..	....
126¼	**Lancaster**	6 19	2 45	..	..	7 45	..	..	..	6 19	..	..	7 45	..	..	..	....

Bradshaw January 1845

London to Preston.
Changing carriages at *6 15 a.m.; in private carriages only at 8¾† a.m.; in the same carriage 10 a.m. mail, and *8½ p.m. mail.
From Birmingham in the same carriage at *1 10 a.m. and *2¼ p.m., changing carriages at *11¼ a.m.
† These trains will take private carriages and horse boxes, the others cannot do so. * Second class carriages accompany these trains.

Bradshaw's Guide for January 1845 contained this data to help those wishing to travel over the route.

London, Oxford, Rugby, Tamworth, Stafford, Shrewsbury, Birmingham, Wolverhampton, Crewe, Manchester, Huddersfield, Chester, Holyhead, Warrington, Liverpool, Fleetwood, and Scotland.—London and North Western.

Supt. of the Line, G. P. Neele, Euston.   General Manager, George Findlay, Euston.   Sec. S. Reay, Euston.   Chief Eng., F. Stevenson, C.E., Euston.

WEEK DAYS.

Station		
Victoria (Brighton)		
" (District)		
Kensington		
Broad Street (City)		
EUSTON		
Willesden Junction		
Sudbury & Wembley		
Harrow		
Pinner		
Bushey		
Watford		
King's Langley		
Boxmoor, fr Hemel Hmp.		
Berkhamsted (fr Chshm)		
Tring (for Wendover)		
Cheddington		
Cheddington dep		
Marston Gate		
Aylesbury		
Leighton		
Leighton dep		
Stanbridgeford		
Dunstable arr		
Bletchley arr		
CAMBRIDGE dep		
OXFORD (Rooly Rd)		
BANBRY (Meltn Rd)		
Bletchley		
Wolverton (for Stoney)		
Castlethorpe (Stratford)		
Roade		
Blisworth		
Northampton (Castle Station) dep		
Althorp Park		
Long Buckby		
Kilsby and Crick		
Weedon (for Daventry)		
Welton (for Guilsbro')		
Rugby arr		
Leamington arr		
Rugby dep		
Brinklow		
Shilton		
Bulkington		
LEICESTER dep		
Nuneaton		
Atherstone		
Polesworth		
Tamworth		
Lichfield		
Armitage		
Rugeley Junction		
Colwich		
Milford and Brocton		
Stafford arr		

Bradshaw September 1885

LONDON, RUGBY, BIRMINGHAM, WOLVERHAMPTON, STAFFORD, SHREWSBURY, CREWE, MANCHESTER, CHESTER, NORTH WALES, IRELAND, LIVERPOOL, WARRINGTON, PRESTON, CARLISLE, and SCOTLAND.—L. & N. W.

Dist. Goods Man., L. A. P. Warner, Waterloo Stn., Liverpool. Dist. Goods Man., R. F. Castleman, Crewe. Dist. Pass. Supt., Southern Division, L. W. Horne.

Down.

Week Days—Continued.

FIVE
Services
Each Way
Daily.
—
IRELAND
AND
ENGLAND
VIA
HOLYHEAD.

EUSTON .... dep.
Broad Street "
Willesden Junction "
Watford "
King's Langley **D** "
Boxmoor "
Berkhamsted "
Tring "
Cheddington 441 "
Leighton 435 "
Bletchley 440, 441 .... arr.
441 CAMBRIDGE .... dep.
440 OXFORD (Rewley Rd) "
Bletchley .... dep.
Wolverton **J** 430 "
Castlethorpe "
Roade "
Blisworth 442 .... arr.
Northampton { (Castle) 369, 444 } dep.
Blisworth "
Weedon 439 "
Welton "
Althorp Park "
Long Buckby "
Kilsby and Crick "
Rugby 443, 448, 489 .. arr.
449 LEAMINGTON ‖ 489 "
448 COVENTRY .... "
448 BIRMINGHAM §§ .. "
454 WALSALL .... "
450 DUDLEY .... "
454 WOLVERHAMPTON "
448 LEAMINGTON 489 ..
434 COVENTRY 448, 449
Rugby ....
Brinklow, for Stretton-Shilton .. [under-Fosse
Bulkington **Y** , 446, 572.
Nuneaton 434, 445 .. arr.
445 LEICESTER (Lon. Rd). dp
Nuneaton .... dep.
Atherstone "
Polesworth "
Tamworth 572, 579 "
Lichfield (Trent Val.) 447 "
Armitage "
Rugeley (Trent Valley) 445 "
Colwich 533 "
Milford and Brocton "
Stafford 373, 462, 533 .. arr.
450 BIRMINGHAM (N.S.) ..
447 WALSALL "
450 DUDLEY "
450 WOLVERHAMPTON "
450 STAFFORD " .... arr.
456 SHREWSBURY 462 .. arr.
Stafford ....
Great Bridgeford "
Norton Bridge **A** 533 "
533 STOKE .... arr.
533 MACCLESFIELD "
Standon Bridge "
Whitmore "
Madeley ... [**530**
Betley Road ... [486, 516,
Crewe 103, 456, 472 .. arr.
516 STOCKPORT 520 .. arr.
446 BUXTON 526 "
516 MANCHESTER (L.R.) "
528 (Vic.) "
488 BOLTON †† 774 "
501 BLACKBURN 766 "
514 OLDHAM (Clegg St.) "
514 ROCHDALE "
520 HUDDERSFIELD "
520 LEEDS (New) "
472 CHESTER "
480 BIRKENHEAD * "
472 RHYL "
472 COLWYN BAY "
472 LLANDUDNO "
472 BANGOR "
472 HOLYHEAD "
472 DUBLIN "
914 BELFAST 920 "
Crewe .... dep.
Minshull Vernon "
Winsford **Z** "
Hartford **X** 528 "
Acton Bridge 488 "
Runcorn ...... [780
Liverpool (L. St.) 483, ar
Preston Brook "
Moore "
Warrington ‡ 420, 502 ar
Earlestown Junc. 496 "
496 ST. HELENS ‡‡ "
Newton-le-Willows 494 arr.
Wigan **V** 420, 756 .. arr.
756 SOUTHPORT (C. St.) .. arr.
Preston 420, 742, 758 ar
758 BLACKPOOL (T.R.) .. "
758 (Cen.) "
758 FLEETWOOD "
758 BELFAST "
Lancaster (Castle) 420 arr.
420 WINDERMERE .... arr.
Carlisle 420, 830, 848 arr.
848 EDINBRO' (Princs St) arr
848 GLASGOW (Central) "
849 PERTH "
849 DUNDEE (West) "
849 INVERNESS "
849 ABERDEEN "

⁎ Tourists travelling to Stirling, Callander, Oban, Perth, Dundee, and Inverness can go via Edinburgh, breaking their journey there, see page xxii.

Bradshaw July 1910

III. The Grand Junction Railway (GJR) of 1837 was the first to serve Crewe, which was designated a First Class Station. It was situated where the railway intersected the Nantwich to Sandbach turnpike, later the A534. The location is close to the entrance to Crewe Hall, marked by the word Lodge, from which the station took its name. This in turn was the surname of the family for whom the hall was completed in 1636. In 2017, the Grade 1 listed building was an upmarket hotel, restaurant and spa. The population of the district that became Crewe was estimated in 1831 as 70; in 1901 the town's inhabitants numbered 42,074, and, in 2011, 71,722. Its remarkable growth in the 19th century was almost entirely attributable to the coming of the railway. It is the archetypal railway town.

The straight alignment of the GJR route is apparent in this map of 1911, scaled at 6ins to 1 mile. Crewe Station expanded as it became a junction for lines to Chester and Manchester, north of the platforms, and Stoke and Shrewsbury at the south end. It reached its zenith between 1901 and 1985, when 16 platforms were in operation. To the left of the station, and at a lower level, are the Independent lines, which date from the 1895-1902 re-modelling, and which were built for freight traffic to avoid the busy station area. These largely survived in 2017. The Up Liverpool Independent line can be seen leaving the GJR next to the Alexandra Athletic Grounds, and tunneling beneath Crewe North Junction. Adjacent to the station is the Crewe Arms Hotel, the first railway hotel in the world, which opened in 1840 and continued to fulfill its original purpose in 2017.

[continued opposite]

The three rail connected buildings north west of the station are Crewe North motive power depot (5A), one of the country's largest steam sheds, until eliminated by the march of progress in 1965. Crewe North Junction has the Chester line heading westward, and the Manchester line of 1842 north eastwards.

The original line to Chester, of 1840, diverges just beyond its successor and passes north of High Street. This remained in use for workmens' trains until 1989. The second Chester line is a deviation of 1868 passing over Mill Street, realigned to permit expansion to the locomotive works. These were established in the vee of the junction between the GJR and the original Chester lines in 1840, by transferring operations from the Liverpool & Manchester Railway's site at Edge Hill, which was already becoming cramped. Following its move, the works became the locomotive new build and repair facility for the entire LNWR. The original Crewe site also soon became constrained, and the new works were built north of the Chester line. In 1864, the Works was the first place in the world to install a steel mill using the continuous Bessemer process, which was south of the Chester line. Over 7,000 steam locos were built between 1843 and 1959, and diesels, including the HST power cars, were produced up to 1982. At its height, before WW1, over 20,000 were employed. Following privatisation of the railways in 1994-97 much of the huge site has been sold and redeveloped. In 2017, what remains is owned by Bombardier UK and deals with component overhauls, mainly bogies, wheels and traction. Complete locos were no longer seen. The Crewe Heritage Centre established itself on part of the Old Works site, formally opening in 1987. North of Earle Street bridge were sidings on both sides of the GJR, primarily dealing with domestic coal.

1. This splendid photograph is dated 1883, evidently taken in the late afternoon of a day in late winter or early spring, and it shows the station after its first major rebuilding, completed in 1867. The view is southward from Crewe North Junction signal box (see picture 50 in *Stafford to Chester*). From left to right we see firstly the Crewe Arms Hotel. The up side has an island platform and overall roof, then come the up and down through lines. The down side has a much wider island platform with a double bay. The outer through line has a separate roof. To the right of that are lines for goods transfers and light engine movements. The footbridge running left to right linked the station with the locoshed. The bridge running off the right hand margin led to the Loco Works and carried part of the 18ins gauge works tramway system. Both bridges were strictly for the sole use of railway staff. The signal box above the through lines was Scissors Crossing Box, which was in use between 1876 and 1958. There is a rake of stock in the left hand bay. (Science Museum/NRM)

2. Probably taken at the same time as the previous picture, this is the view north from Crewe North Junction. The realigned Chester lines go off to the left, the ex-GJR runs straight ahead, and the Manchester lines go right. The original Works complex fills the space between the Chester and GJR routes, with the Works tramway descending from the bridge into the yard. The oldest building, with the clock tower, is adjacent to the GJR. (M.Dart coll.)

3. Looking north from the footbridge in 1937, we see nearly new Black Five no. 5297 arriving at platform 4 from the GJ line with a long train of mostly LNW carriages, probably a relief service. The loco was allocated to Monument Lane at this time, suggesting the train was bound for Birmingham. The Works bridge is seen passing across Crewe North Junction, and then, remarkably, through the middle of North Junction signal box. The Works bridge, often called the Spider Bridge, was in use between 1878 and 1939. The span across North Junction was a suspension bridge; the Chester lines can be seen curving to the left above the first and second vehicles. This version of North Junction signal box was in use between 1906 and 1940. Its interior is illustrated in picture 3 of our *Crewe to Manchester* album. (E.R.Morten/J.Suter coll.)

4. Probably taken on the same day in 1937, LMS 4-4-0 no. 1116 awaits the road with a down train. The loco is painted in lined crimson lake livery and the coaching stock looks brand new. On the loco road to the left is 'Jubilee' class no. 5591 *Udaipur* awaiting the arrival of another down service which it will take forward. We see that the footbridge ends in a ramp leading towards North Shed. The start of the Independent lines' tunnel beneath North Junction is marked by the wall to the right of the bottom of the ramp. (E.R.Morten/J.Suter coll.)

5. A poignant picture taken on 29th August 1952 of 4-6-2 no. 46202 *Princess Anne* at platform 1 working the 8.30am Euston – Liverpool. It was just 11 days fresh from Crewe Works, where it had been rebuilt from the LMS Turbomotive. It ran only until the following 8th October when it was involved in the disastrous double collision at Harrow & Wealdstone and incurred damage that was beyond economic repair. (M.Dart)

6. On 19th August 1955, we look north from the footbridge as no. 46235 *City of Birmingham* runs into platform 4 with the 9.30am Glasgow Central – Birmingham New St. The Pacific has a sloping smokebox top (making it a 'Semi'), having previously been streamlined. It later received a fully rounded version, and can still be seen in 2017 in its final form at Thinktank, the Birmingham Science Museum. The 'Spider Bridge' has been removed, opening up the view. This uncluttered scene lasted only until 1958, when the first masts for overhead electrification were erected. The platform is in the process of receiving an extended canopy. Above it, we get a glimpse of North Locoshed, which is unable to entirely conceal the massive coaling plant; a 'Princess Royal' Pacific is in the shed yard with what may be an ex-LNWR 0-8-0. Above the first carriage is Crewe North Junction signal box, built in concrete and flat roofed, which replaced the one seen in picture 3 in 1940. It was taken out of use in 1985, but in 2017 it remained in situ as a key attraction of Crewe Heritage Centre. Behind that is the original Crewe Locomotive Works, which by this time was the boiler repair shop. (B.Morrison)

7. BR 'Pacific' no. 71000 *Duke of Gloucester* was both a Standard and unique. It was authorised as a replacement for no. 46202 (picture 5), and was just one year old when this picture was taken, also on Friday 19th August 1955. It was taken out of traffic only seven years later. Thankfully, it survives in preservation and operates main line steam specials. Here it is on the down through road with the 1.45pm Birmingham New Street – Manchester London Road. To the right is platform 2, the easterly side of the third island platform, which was added in the second enlargement of the station, completed in 1906 after 10 years of work. To the left is platform 3, the most westerly part of the 1867 station. Above the train can be seen the station entrance on the Nantwich Road bridge. (B.Morrison)

8. Crewe was not just about big engines. On Saturday 20th August 1955, class 2MT 2-6-2T no. 41229 stands at the end of bay platform 3A with the 12.52pm Northwich motor train. The adjacent platform 4A is temporarily closed whilst a new canopy is erected, replacing a section of the overall roof which has been removed. To the right of the loco is a water crane for the topping up of thirsty boilers, and a brazier to keep the water supply from freezing in cold weather. Right of this the tail of an express stands in platform 3, evidently GWR stock so probably bound for the south west. Over 20 spotters can be counted on the footbridge – those were the days! (B.Morrison)

9. In this view from 5th July 1962, the photographer has stood in more or less exactly the same place as for picture 8, and what a transformation! Overhead electrification at 25kV AC has been implemented, and all steam infrastructure has disappeared from view (although steam continued here until late 1967). The platforms have been resurfaced, and the wall between platforms 3A and 3 which once supported the ends of two overall roofs has been demolished, along with the footbridge. The station entrance has been rebuilt. Consecutively numbered AM4 (later class 304) EMUs occupy platforms 3A and 4A. These 4-coach sets were initially painted Brunswick Green with yellow warning panels at either end. To the right an AL5 electric loco has come onto the front of a down service to Liverpool or Manchester at platform 2. (D.K.Jones)

Further pictures of Crewe station can be seen in the *Crewe to Manchester,* *Shrewsbury to Crewe,* **and** *Stafford to Chester* **albums from Middleton Press.**

10. We are standing on platform 4 at 15.43 on 7th April 1973 as Co-Co nos 444 and 401 arrive with the 12.00 Glasgow Central – London Euston. Fifty of these 2700hp diesels, later class 50, were built in 1967-68 for the West Coast Main Line, which was not electrified north of Crewe until the summer of 1973, being used in pairs for the Anglo-Scottish services. They will be uncoupled and replaced by an electric loco for the last 158 miles to Euston. The heart of the station retains much of its 1950s character, with maroon backed signage, well-stocked newspaper kiosk, and the departures listed at the foot of the stairs on a long scroll in a tall cabinet. The buildings on both platforms date from the 1867 rebuilding, and still served in 2017. Platforms 1 to 6 served the through lines; the platform on the right is number 5. Bay platforms were suffixed A (north end) or B (south end). (T.Heavyside)

11. The trackwork through Crewe station was remodelled in 1985. The elimination of such archaic activities as changing locomotives and wagon load freight meant the layout was ripe for simplification, and the number of platforms could be reduced. The axe fell on most of the third island platform dating from 1906; the track was removed from the outer face (platform 1) and all four bay lines. The inner through line (platform 2) was retained. At the same time the remaining platforms were renumbered 1 – 12 from east to west with the bay platforms having separate numbers. On 25th February 1995, no. 87028 *Lord President* leaves platform 11 (the old number 3) with the 10.00 London Euston – Liverpool Lime Street. To the extreme left is platform 5 (the only one which did not change its number in 1985), then number 6 (old number 4). Platform 9 (old 4A) is occupied by DMU no. 156440 forming the 12.24 to Bangor; the canopy is the one we saw under construction in picture 8. The track from platform 12 (old number 2) trails in ahead of the locomotive. To the right is the end ramp of old platform 1A, now trackless, with the footbridge over the old number 1 road giving access to Crewe Signalling Control Centre, which replaced the remaining local signal boxes in 1985. The station frontage seen in the background was subsequently replaced. (A.C.Hartless)

12. A final view of the east side from 8th September 2012 sees no. 66058 running through platform 1 (old number 6) with the 12.18 Willesden – Tunstead cement empties. The Crewe Arms Hotel is recognisably the 1840 building plus some extension. Note also the wall with decorative arches starting behind the second wagon, and compare with picture 1. The rear of a class 350 'Desiro' EMU can be seen at platform 5 running from Liverpool to Birmingham. (P.D.Shannon)

Crewe North Shed

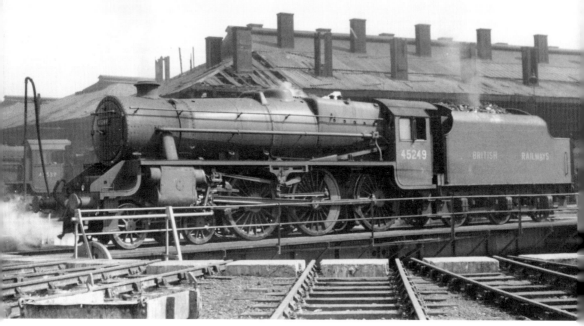

13. On 28th April 1951, 'Black Five' no. 45249, a visitor from Holyhead, is turned for its return journey. Note the loco's early style of British Railways livery, also the precarious state of the shed roof. (H.C.Casserley)

14. On 20th August 1955, 'Patriot' class 4-6-0 no. 45503 *The Royal Leicestershire Regiment* is ready for the road with its tender stacked high with coal. Note the reporting number board resting on the front of the tender before being fitted to the smokebox door. (B.Morrison)

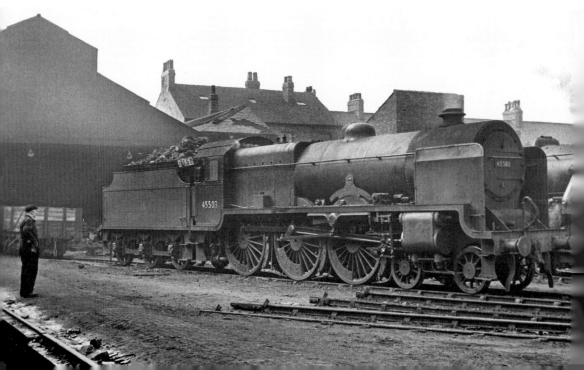

15. The first of the LMS 'Pacifics', no. 46200 *The Princess Royal*, is inside the middle shed on 9th September 1962. It is receiving a piston and valve exam, which were usually performed here on the 4-6-2s. A battered fitters' bench stands in the foreground next to the inspection pit. The loco was withdrawn only two months later after 29 years of service. (Colour Rail/K.Field)

Other pictures of Shed 5A can be seen in *Stafford to Chester*.

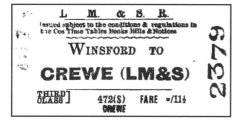

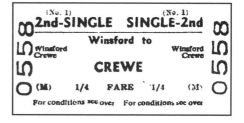

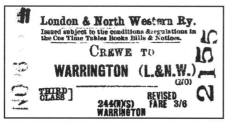

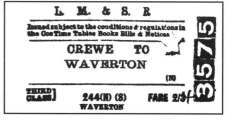

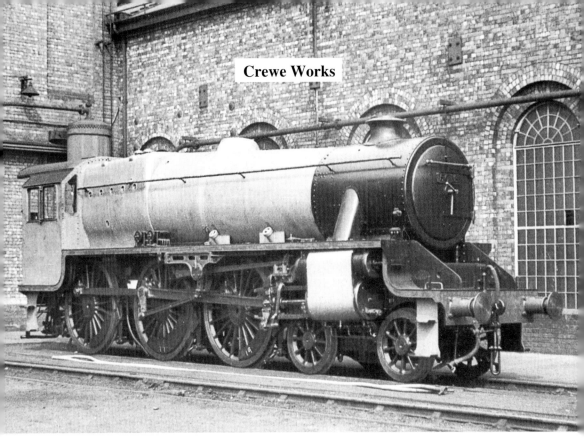

16. Built at Crewe, one of the earliest 5MT 4-6-0 'Black Fives', no. 5018, is awaiting painting and its tender in April 1935. It ran in service until the end of 1966. (A.C.Hartless coll)

17. We have already seen a portion of the internal 18" gauge tramway in pictures 1 and 2. The system was abandoned in 1929, but one of the locos, *Pet*, was saved and kept in a corner of the Old Works for some 30 years before becoming a founding item of the National Collection. In 2017, it could be seen at the National Railway Museum. The photograph is dated 19th July 1936. Note the cut lengths of boiler tube in the foreground, whilst behind is a replica of Stepenson's *Rocket*, built in the previous year. Other preserved LNWR locos including *Cornwall* and *Hardwicke* were kept here until the late 1950s. (H.F.Wheeller coll.)

18. The New Works of the 1860s was separated from the Old Works by a tree lined stretch of the original Chester line known as The Dell. Class 8F 2-8-0 no. 48133 is seen there sometime in 1948, as a party of visitors makes its way back to the exit at the Old Works. The W1 board shows the loco is working on one of the internal works shunting turns. These were usually handled by dedicated, and often ancient, engines that never left the works, but this large modern loco is probably being run in, after repair. (B. Brooksbank)

19. In the age old practice of recycling, many of the steam locos built here were subsequently melted down here. It so happened in 1949 that the last three LNWR passenger locos were taken out of traffic around the same time. They were assembled for final photographs, and then sadly all scrapped. On 19th June 1949, the melancholy line up was 'Precursor' 4-4-0 no. 25297 *Sirocco*, built in 1904, 'Claughton' 4-6-0 no. 6004, built in 1921 and originally named *Princess Louise*, and 'Prince of Wales' 4-6-0 no. 25752, built in 1919. (R.J.Buckley/Initial Photographics)

20. Here is no. 45500 fresh out of the paint shop at the end of an overhaul, sometime in 1957. This was the first of 52 locos to this design, and it entered traffic in 1930. It was given the name *Patriot In Memory of the Fallen L&NWR Employees 1914-1919* in 1937 after the original bearer of the name, 'Claughton' no. 5964, was scrapped. The class was thenceforward officially known as the 'Patriot' class. The last of the design was withdrawn in 1962 and all were scrapped. In 2017, construction of a new build Patriot to be called *The Unknown Warrior* was well advanced and the aim was to have the loco running in time for the centenary of the WW1 Armistice on 11 November 2018. (R.S.Carpenter coll.)

Stafford to Chester **contains other pictures of Crewe Works and also Crewe Heritage Centre.**

21. In the post steam era, repaired locos were tested before being released to traffic, rather than run in on the main line. Four locomotives are evident on 19th August 1973. Co-Co diesel no. 431, a Brush Type 4 and two AL6 electrics are in the test area. The former has evidently just emerged from the paint shop in the right background, and will have used the traverser in the foreground to reach its current position. (F.Hornby)

NORTH OF CREWE

Coppenhall Junction

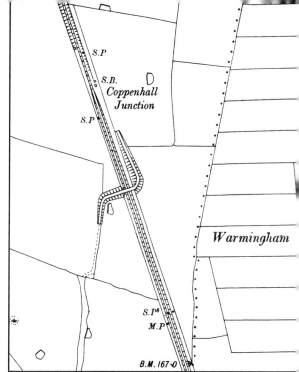

IV. The GJR had a short-lived station at Coppenhall, 1½ miles north of Crewe, from its opening until 10th September 1840. Its early closure was attributable to opening of the Chester line three weeks later and the concentration of local passenger facilities at the newly created junction of Crewe. The GJR was quadrupled for 3 miles in 1908 north of Crewe to a point called Coppenhall Junction, which was situated in deep countryside, as shown on this 7ins to 1 mile map of 1908. It was only ever a junction as the end of quadruple track between 1908 - 1927, after which the route was four tracked as far as Winsford. There were crossovers here until 1979.

MINSHULL VERNON

Vimboldsley Hall

V. Minshull Vernon was almost five miles of straight and mostly level track from Crewe. It was where the railway was crossed by the Nantwich to Middlewich turnpike, which became the A530 in 1919. Minshull Vernon is the name of a rural parish, of which Church Minshull, to the south west, is the main settlement. The station was sited in open countryside close to Wimboldsley Hall. The 25ins map shows the status in 1908, before the line was quadrupled in 1927 between Coppenhall Junction and Winsford, and the station was rebuilt. Nevertheless, it was closed from 2nd March 1942, because of poor patronage. The platforms, serving only the two outer tracks, remained until 1961, when the line was electrified. There was never any facility for goods.

22. An up express runs through sometime in the first five years of the 20th century. Note the milk churns awaiting collection – this is prime dairy country. Milk continued to be collected by rail from nearby Calveley, on the Chester line, until the 1960s. (P.A.Laming coll.)

23. Seen from more or less the same position, on Saturday 16th August 1958, a pair of Black Fives lead the 10.10am Edinburgh Princes Street – Birmingham New Street, made up of 17 coaches. The pilot loco is no. 44750, one of the sub-class with Caprotti valve gear. Compared with the previous picture, the down platform is in the same place, but the up side has been moved to accommodate two extra tracks. The bridge has been rebuilt, and a new station building provided on the right. By 1958 this was used by Permanent Way staff, and lasted another 15 years or so.
(E.R.Morten/J.Suter coll.)

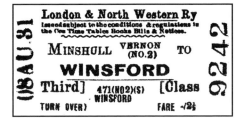

24. Looking the other way on the same day, no. 46115 *Scots Guardsman* is going well northbound with another heavy train. This loco was destined to be the last 'Royal Scot' in service, being withdrawn at the end of 1965, and survives in preservation as a main line performer. The signal box closed in 1961, when electrification and resignalling were implemented. (E.R.Morten/J.Suter coll.)

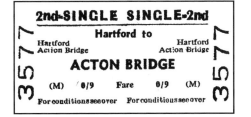

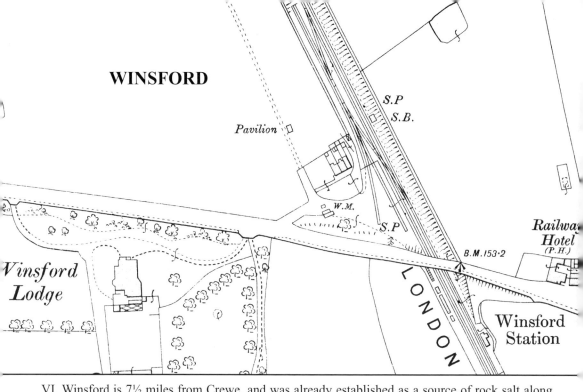

WINSFORD

Pavilion

S.P
S.B.

W.M.

S.P

B.M.153·2

Vinsford Lodge

Railway Hotel (P.H.)

L O N D O N

Winsford Station

VI. Winsford is 7½ miles from Crewe, and was already established as a source of rock salt along the Weaver Valley before the arrival of the railway. The GJR passed one mile to the east of the town where it was crossed by the road to Middlewich, later the A54. The 1909 map, at 25ins to 1 mile, shows a siding to the north of the bridge; this was primarily a coal yard and closed in the late 1950s. Winsford Station signal box closed in 1927 when quadruple track reached Winsford South Junction, some 30 chains south of the station. From there to Winsford Junction, there have only ever been two tracks. In 2017, Winsford, with a population of 33,000, was still the site of Britain's largest rock salt mine, which also claims to be the country's oldest continuously working mine of any sort, dating from 1844. The town has diversified since the mid 20th century, and has the HQs for Cheshire West & Chester Council and the Cheshire Police and Fire Services.

25. An up passenger train comes under the bridge in around 1905. The down side building has provision for gentlemen. Another milk churn is on display along with gas lighting. (P.A.Laming coll.)

26. Seen from a down stopper on 10th October 1959, the main up side building of 1837 is identical to the original one at Minshull Vernon. The low window sills reflect the increase in the height of the platform over the intervening 122 years. The sign for the Gents largely obscures that for the Ladies' Waiting Room. No doubt the bike shed and lamp room are later additions. (H.C.Casserley)

27. The station was completely rebuilt ahead of electrification in 1960/61. New modular buildings of a type used widely in the WCML modernisation were provided. The A54 road bridge was replaced allowing the necessary clearance for the overhead wires, and also for future quadrupling. A footbridge linking the platforms was constructed. On 3rd July 1976, class 304 EMU no. 045 arrives with the 14.37 Liverpool Lime Street – Crewe. These units worked the locals on this route for over 30 years. Compared with the two sets seen in picture 9, the mid-1970s livery was Rail Blue with full yellow ends. Headcodes were no longer displayed by this time. Note also the flared jeans then in vogue. (T.Heavyside)

28. The 1961 waiting shelters became life expired much sooner than the steam age buildings they replaced, and were rebuilt in more durable materials with a far less attractive appearance. On 25th February 1988, no. 58042 *Ironbridge Power Station* passes with a rake of empty HAA coal wagons returning from Garston Dock to one of the East Midlands collieries, its outward load having been shipped to Northern Ireland for power generation. The 50 class 58 diesels were built in the mid 1980s for coal traffic, which was destined to fall away rapidly in the following decade. (T.Heavyside)

OVER & WHARTON

➜   VIIa. The left map, scale approx 4ins to 1 mile, shows the branch in 1938. The GJR had been open for only three years when the first connections to the Weaver Valley salt works were made. The branch line was extended in stages, serving two industrial complexes on the east bank of the river, before reaching the new passenger terminus and goods station on 1st June 1882, completing a branch of 1¼ miles. The engine shed nearest the terminus was LNWR property, the one further north belonged to the salt works. Over, the oldest part of Winsford, was granted a weekly market by Royal Charter in 1280, and forms the westernmost part of the town; Wharton is east of the river.

Winsford Junction signal box was located at Key's Crossing, with the start of the branch, and its associated sidings, ¼ mile to the south. The one mile section of the main line northwards to Verdin Sidings, where there were further salt workings, was quadrupled in 1898 and reverted to double track in the early 1970s.

➜➜   VIIb. The right map is 25ins to 1 mile. It is from 1909 and shows the terminus in detail.

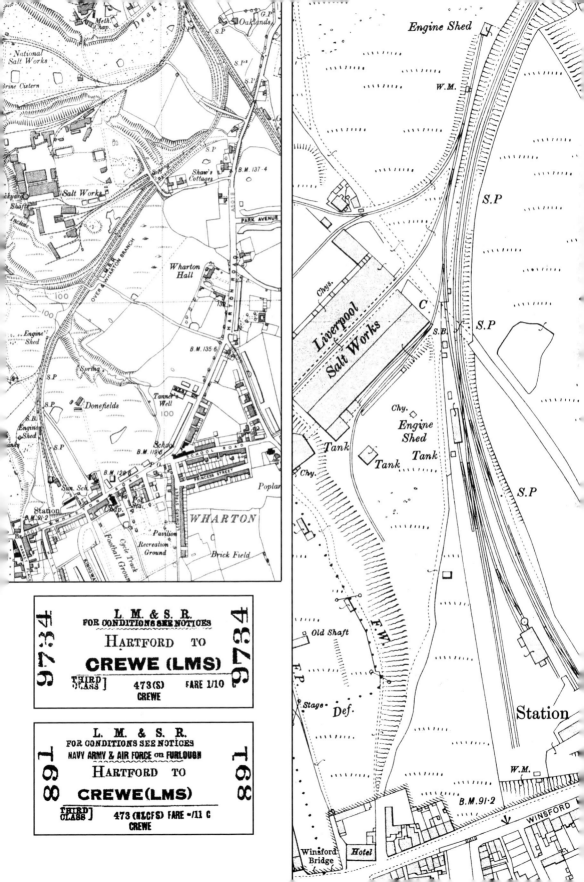

29. On 14th June 1947, ex LNWR 0-6-2T no. 6906 replenishes its water tanks at the loco shed. The one-road building had lost half of its roof; a second loco can be seen inside. The shed closed some 10 weeks later, but stood, along with the water tower, until around 1967, when steam ended here. The signal box lasted only until 1952. The line running through the gate went to one of the salt works, and the branch goes out of the picture on the right. (W.A.Camwell)

30. Saturday 14th June 1947 was the last day of the passenger service. No. 6906 has moved to the terminus and waits in the afternoon sun with the final train to Warrington. The single storey passenger station is at right angles to the train fronting Wharton Road. The goods yard is on the far right. This closed from 10th June 1968, but salt traffic continued until early 1990, after which the branch was lifted. Almost all the trackbed was used for a deviation of the A5018, Wharton Park Road. (W.A.Camwell)

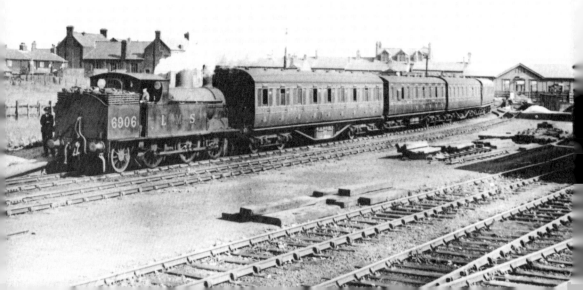

31. Only one track of the branch was required after 1952. Many branches in a similar position were used in the late 50s for the storage of surplus wagons, but in 1959 and 1960 the Over & Wharton line was used for storing redundant steam locos destined for scrap at Crewe. Sometime in the Spring of 1959 ex-LNWR 0-8-0 no. 49109, recently withdrawn from Speke Junction shed, is one of at least a dozen in the temporary dump. (Colour-Rail)

32. The last steam hauled passenger train on the branch was an enthusiasts' special on 23rd April 1966. 2MT 2-6-0 no. 78036 stands at the terminus having propelled its six coach train from Winsford Junction. It had come onto the train at Wellington and reached here via Market Drayton and the Crewe Independent lines. (Colour-Rail)

33. On 3rd April 1991, DVT no. 82114 leads the 09.00 Glasgow – Euston past Winsford signal box, which dates from 1898 and was formally called Winsford Junction. The Over & Wharton branch is in the foreground. In 2017, this was the only intermediate signal box between Crewe and Warrington, controlling the section from Winsford South Junction to Weaver Junction. (RCTS coll.)

34. 'Royal Scot' no. 6165 *The Ranger (12th London Regt)* heads north between Verdin Sidings and Vale Royal Viaduct in June 1934. All of the 'Scots' were later rebuilt with tapered boilers. (E.R.Morten/J.Suter coll.)

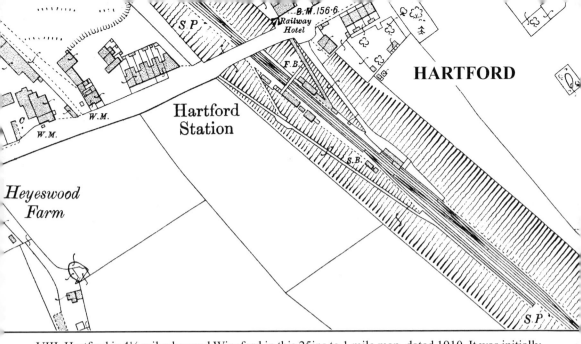

VIII. Hartford is 4¼ miles beyond Winsford in this 25ins to 1 mile map, dated 1910. It was initially the nearest station to Chester (15 miles away) and Northwich (2½), being located where the former Roman military road from Chester to Manchester, now the A559, crosses the route. The village had a population of 950 in 1851, which rose to 5515 in 2001. The section from Verdin Siding to Hartford Junction has only ever been two tracked. To the south of Hartford, the line crosses the River Weaver by Vale Royal Viaduct, a five arched structure 60ft high made from local stone, and then runs through a long cutting in which the station is located. Because of space constraint, the goods station was a single road shed on the up side immediately south of the platform. The goods yard closed from 17th August 1959 when local goods traffic was concentrated at nearby Greenbank (featured in *Chester to Manchester*). The siding on the down side north of the station was a coal yard which also closed in 1959.

35. This delightful postcard was franked on 10th March 1908. The approaching train is an up goods hauled by a class B 0-8-0 compound. The main up side building and the open fronted shelter are markedly similar to those at Winsford, with the exception of the tall chimney stacks. The down side building here is of similar size to the up one, suggesting passengers were just as likely to travel north as south. Covered steps lead to the road on the up side, and the platforms are linked by a footbridge. The depth of the cutting is emphasised by the height of the road bridge's graceful arch. (P.A.Laming coll.)

36. Now we look south in 1957 as class 8F 2-8-0 no. 48291 passes with a down goods. Note the small goods shed and siding on the up side, and on the down the signal box and another siding beyond. All this was swept away by electrification. The signal box was the last surviving by signalling contractors Saxby & Farmer on the former GJR main line, and dated from 1876. (H.B.Priestley)

37. On 22nd May 1961, 'Patriot' no. 45543 *Home Guard* calls with a down local. The rebuilding of the station is well underway using a larger version of the modular shelters seen at Winsford; the platforms have been extended and the goods station removed. Overhead electrification has been erected, but not yet energised. Mechanical signalling clings on for a short while longer. (B.Brooksbank)

38. On 15th April 1993, everything looks in good order as no. 31421 *Wigan Pier* runs in with the 13.22 Crewe – Liverpool. The 1961 rebuilding relocated booking facilities adjacent to the replacement footbridge instead of at street level. (T.Heavyside)

39. On 25th October 2010, a class 221 Virgin Trains Super Voyager runs through with the 13.00 Glasgow – Birmingham. The graceful arch remains, aided by strengthening rods. The afternoon sun picks out the Mid Cheshire railway bridge some 35 chains further north. (A.C.Hartless)

NORTH OF HARTFORD

Hartford Junction

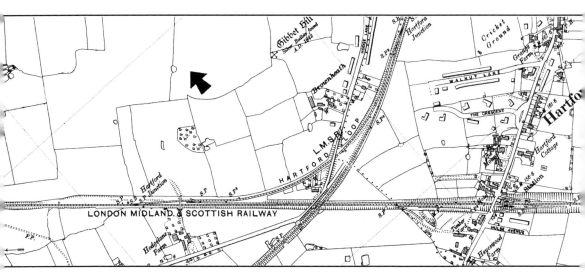

IX. Our route runs from right to left and the LNER Mid Cheshire line (featured in *Chester to Manchester*) from bottom to top, in this 1938 map scaled at 4ins to 1 mile. The latter opened in 1869 and the Hartford Loop linkng the two was opened in March 1870 by the LNWR, which had running powers to Northwich. The modern name for Hartford Junction on the Mid Cheshire line is Hartford CLC Junction. The loop continues to be a useful link for freight between the Northwich area, and Runcorn and Warrington. Hartford Junction is roughly one mile from Hartford Station.

40. On 12th April 1966, class 8F 2-8-0 no. 48255 rolls down the Hartford Loop with soda ash empties. The Mid Cheshire line is in the background. (B.Brooksbank)

41. No. 40158 approaches Hartford Junction on 5th April 1983 with a Northwich – Warrington freight, consisting of empty coal wagons, the tail of which is passing beneath Hodge Lane bridge in the background. This point also marks the limit of electrification on the loop. (A.C.Hartless)

42. Looking in the opposite direction on 16th April 1983, no. 86227 *Sir Henry Johnson* runs up the main line with the 11.25 Liverpool – Euston. The track in the foreground is the up slow, which was installed between Acton Bridge and here in 1927. Hartford Junction signal box is just visible above the second coach; this was in use between 1927 and 1994. Going out of the picture to the right is the Hartford Loop, initially a single line, but turning to double track. In the right background are the reception sidings at the south end of Gorstage Yard, with connections to both our route and the Loop. (A.C.Hartless)

X. Gorstage Yard was opened in 1953 on the up side between Hartford Junction and Acton Bridge. It was owned by Imperial Chemical Industries (ICI) and comprised eight long sidings connected to the newly constructed two mile long Wallerscote Light Railway. This provided an alternative and less steeply graded rail access to ICI's massive Wallerscote & Winnington complex than that provided from the Mid Cheshire line. At the south end of the yard were three further sidings belonging to BR. The yard and the light railway were taken out of use in the early 1990s following the closure of the Wallerscote factory. The map is at 2ins to 1 mile as revised in 1964. The Wallerscote Light Railway leaves Gorstage Yard running eastwards before passing beneath the B5153 to reach ICI's Wallerscote/ Winnington complex above the word NORTHWICH. The main product of the works was soda ash (sodium carbonate), used in the manufacture of glass, paper, detergents and as a water softener.

Gorstage Yard

43. On 26th May 1936, 'Prince of Wales' class 4-6-0 no. 25673 *Lusitania* heads a mixed rake up the fast line across Gorstage Lane bridge. The northern limit of the yard was constructed to the right of the loco. (E.R.Morten/J.Suter coll.)

44. ICI produced a publicity brochure to mark the opening of the new facilities in February 1953, which included this southward view of the yard. The Wallerscote Light Railway is on the left, whilst an unrebuilt 'Royal Scot' is heading a down express at right. ICI's locomotive fleet here included five 400hp 0-6-0 diesel shunters of similar appearance to the LMS designed nos 12033 – 12138 series, later BR class 10. (ICI/A.C.Hartless coll.)

45. On 16th April 1983, no. 86232 *Harold Macmillan* passes the three BR reception and despatch sidings at the south end of Gorstage Yard with the 08.50 Euston – Liverpool. Activity in the yard is in decline, and the bothy, for the rest and relaxation of railway staff, stands derelict. (A.C.Hartless)

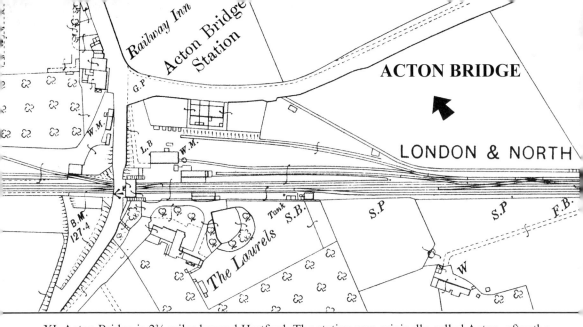

XI. Acton Bridge is 2¾ miles beyond Hartford. The station was originally called Acton, after the village half a mile to the north, but was renamed from 1st July 1870, presumably to avoid confusion with its namesake in West London, which ultimately had seven stations. The 1910 map, scaled at 25ins to 1 mile, shows the trackwork before 1925, with a down loop ending adjacent to the signal box, three sidings on the up side, one ending in the goods shed, fusing into an up loop, and two private sidings on the up side beyond the bridge. In 1925, the sidings were remodelled to commence the up loop north of the bridge, turning the up platform into an island so that up local passenger trains could terminate here, clear of the main lines. And in 1927 the up and down loops were extended to Hartford Jct. This remained the arrangement of the running lines in 2017, although the goods station closed from 4th January 1965. L.B. indicates a letter box.

46. This northward view is probably from the 1900s. The booking office is at street level, spanning the two running lines. The up side building appears to consist of a brick shell with a timber and glass frontage, whilst the down side's is a typical LNWR modular timber construction with brick chimneys. The goods station is behind the up platform; in the yard are four small offices for competing coal merchants. The Railway Hotel beckons across the street. Note also the gated siding immediately beyond the bridge. (LOSA/J.Suter coll.)

47. This is the view south from the footbridge that came with the 1925 widening, which also turned the old up platform into an island with the addition of a third track on the left. The up side building was demolished and replaced by a partitioned canopy, by now in need of repair. The train standing at the down platform is the North Staffs Railtour (part 2) of 31st May 1958 organised by the Stephenson Locomotive Society, and which originated from Birmingham. Class 5MT 2-6-0 no. 42939 has arrived from Stoke-on-Trent via a roundabout route, and will shortly return thence tender first by another. Note the signal box, largely obscured by steam.
(R.J.Buckley/Initial Photographics)

48. A view north is from a similar position to picture 46, but taken on 2nd April 1983. The down side platform building has survived. The bridge was rebuilt and the booking office was relocated to the east side of the line in 1925. The goods depot has been cleared. The up side shelter was replaced around the time of electrification by a small waiting room; a corner of its flat roof cum canopy can be seen to the right of the loco's windows. The loco is no. 40015; the English Electric 2,000hp Type 4s, later class 40, were in the vanguard of dieselisation of services on this line from 1959 and stayed around until the last were withdrawn in 1985. By now, passenger work was limited to special trains; this is a Liverpool – Nottingham footex for the Nottingham Forest vs Everton fixture in the old First Division, which Forest won 2-0. (A.C.Hartless)

49. Nos 90045 and 90043 haul the well loaded 12.13 Daventry - Coatbridge Freightliner service on 5th May 2017. The platform structures are now basic shelters, although the booking office still remains. (P.D.Shannon)

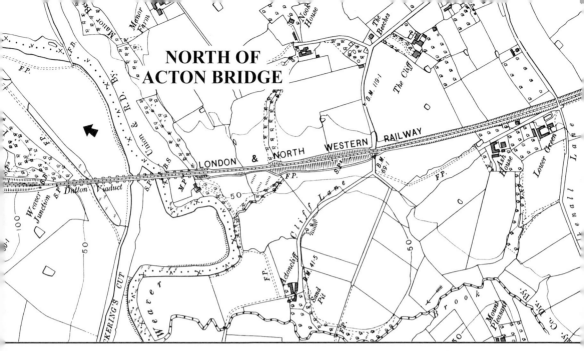

XII. After 1½ miles of double track from Acton Bridge, the route reaches Dutton Viaduct by which it crosses the River Weaver for the second time. The viaduct is 484 yards long comprising 20 arches, the highest being 65ft, making an impressive monument to Joseph Locke and the men who built it from local stone in the mid 1830s. At the time of its construction it was the longest railway viaduct in the world. It was built within budget and its construction incurred neither any fatalities nor serious injuries. It was built to last. When the Runcorn Branch was opened by the LNWR in 1869, it reduced the distance for rail travellers between Crewe and Liverpool by approximately eight miles. The junction was made immediately north of Dutton Viaduct, where Weaver Junction signal box was located on the down side. The Liverpool and Warrington lines then ran parallel for 1¼ miles before separating at Birdswood. The junction was moved around half a mile further north in 1961, and the signal box was relocated. This 1908 map is scaled at 5ins to 1 mile.

Dutton Viaduct

50. In the summer of 1949, no. 46225 *Duchess of Gloucester*, in early BR black livery, heads a 15-coach northbound express. (R.A.Whitfield/RailPhotoprints.uk)

51. In the evening of 8th June 2013, a Virgin Pendolino is heading northwards. The only change to the structure in the intervening 64 years is the addition of electrification gantries. (P.D.Shannon)

Weaver Junction

52. Weaver Junction is seen in the summer of 1949 as a down Anglo-Scottish express takes the main line behind black liveried 'Princess Royal' 4-6-2 no. 46205 *Princess Victoria*. The other four tracks are, from left to right, up goods loop, up Runcorn (on which a train is signalled), up Grand Junction, and down Runcorn. Weaver Junction signal box overlooks the rear of the train, beyond which can be seen the end of the down side parapet of Dutton Viaduct.
(R.A.Whitfield/RailPhotoprints.uk)

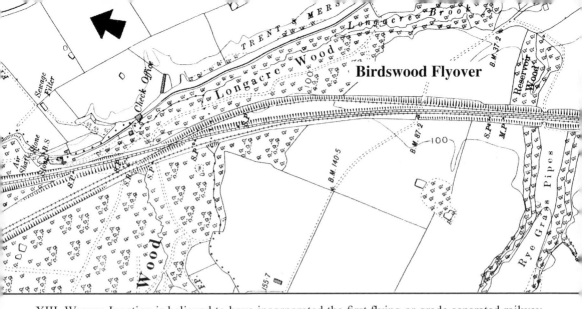

Birdswood Flyover

XIII. Weaver Junction is believed to have incorporated the first flying or grade separated railway junction in the world, where the up Runcorn line is carried across the main lines by a bridge, the Birdswood Flyover, instead of a flat crossing. At the left of this 1908 map (scaled at 8ins to 1 mile), the Runcorn Branch, shown as two single tracks, is the lower of the two routes. Note also the Trent & Mersey Canal east of the railway. In 2017, the line from Crewe to here is still officially called the Crewe and Birdswood Line (Grand Junction), thence to Warrington the Birdswood and Warrington Line, and towards Liverpool the Runcorn Branch.

53. Between Weaver Junction and Birdswood Flyover, class 2 2-4-2T LMSR no. 6688 is seen in the summer of 1949 on the down main with an early evening auto train from Acton Bridge to Warrington (and maybe onward to Earlestown and St Helens). Such locals continued until 1965, with more modern power. (R.A.Whitfield/RailPhotoprints.uk)

54. The replacement Weaver Junction signal box of 1961 was located close to Birdswood Flyover, between the up main in front of the box, and the up Runcorn behind it. Seen on 17th April 1983, this modern box was abolished in 1997 and its functions transferred to Winsford, seen in picture 33. (D. Lennon)

55. On 12th April 1958, the prototype 'Deltic' crosses Birdswood Flyover with a Liverpool – Euston express. This highly distinctive (American body style and light blue livery) and highly powered diesel (3300hp) was built by English Electric in 1955 at Preston as a pitch for business from the coming modernisation of British Railways. It was used mostly on the Liverpool – Euston run, but failed to impress senior management of London Midland Region who had obtained the go ahead to electrify London Euston to Liverpool and Manchester. However, the electrification case for the East Coast Main Line was rejected, and 22 Deltics (class 55) were ordered to replace 55 LNER Pacifics. The prototype was taken out of service in early 1961 after a major failure in one of its two engines, and was donated to the Science Museum in 1963. It moved to the National Railway Museum in 1993. (R.A.Whitfield/RailPhotoprints.uk)

56. In June 1962, 'Britannia' 4-6-2 no. 70031 *Byron* runs under the Birdswood Flyover with what appears to be an Edinburgh or Glasgow to Birmingham express. The Crewe to Liverpool route has been electrified; three masts can be seen on the single track up to Runcorn. The overhead was also erected above the Warrington line for ½ mile beyond the flyover; this 'run off' was provided to cater for the eventuality of an electric service being erroneously routed this way, in which case there was power to reverse and regain the correct line. Note the large maroon sign at left pointing northwards. (R.A.Whitfield/RailPhotoprints.uk)

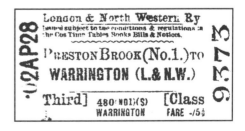

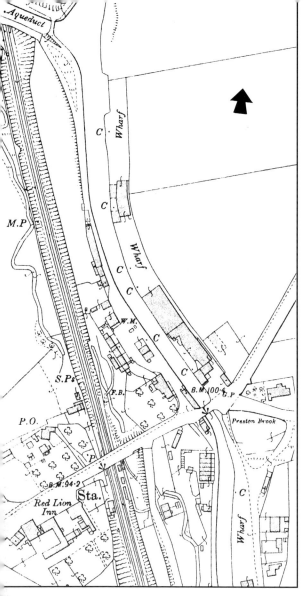

PRESTON BROOK

XIV. Preston Brook was 4 miles from Acton Bridge and 1 from Birdswood Flyover. It was preceded by a cutting around a mile long which included a short tunnel. The goods station was on the up side, with the signal box opposite. The line runs parallel with the Trent & Mersey Canal between Birdswood Flyover and Preston Brook Canal Junction where the T&M linked with the Bridgewater Canal in 1776. This is just to the right of the word 'Aqueduct' near the top margin, which feature carries the canal over the railway. The railway was crossed by the Warrington to Frodsham turnpike, later the A56, immediately north of the station, which was the nearest to Runcorn at the time it opened. The line descended between the station and the aqueduct at 1 in 112, the steepest gradient between Crewe and Warrington. The station closed from 1st March 1948, and goods ceased to be conveyed from 1st September 1958. The M56 motorway runs across the left of a modern day map, spanning the railway and the canal junction. Most of the land west of the railway as far north as the canal has been built over as part of Runcorn New Town. This 1910 map is scaled at 20ins to 1 mile.

57. An early 20th century view of the down side looking north reveals a basic wayside station. The Red Lion Hotel is behind the railings on the left. (A.C.Hartless coll.)

58. An up express hauled by a nearly new streamlined 'Coronation Pacific' shatters the peace in around 1938. The next structure beyond the road bridge is the Bridgewater Canal aqueduct. This was the first structure to be completed on the GJR, and was replaced by a new bridge during the electrification works of the early 1970s. (A.C.Hartless coll.)

59. Preston Brook (aka Dutton) Tunnel is ¾ miles south of the station site. The down 'Royal Scot' emerges one day in 1958 behind the UK's pioneer main line diesels, nos 10000 & 10001, which went into traffic in 1947 & 1948 respectively. The light at the south end of the bore can be seen above the leading coach. The tunnel was 110yds when built, but the southern end collapsed soon after, reducing it to a mere 78yds. (R.A.Whitfield/RailPhotoprints.uk)

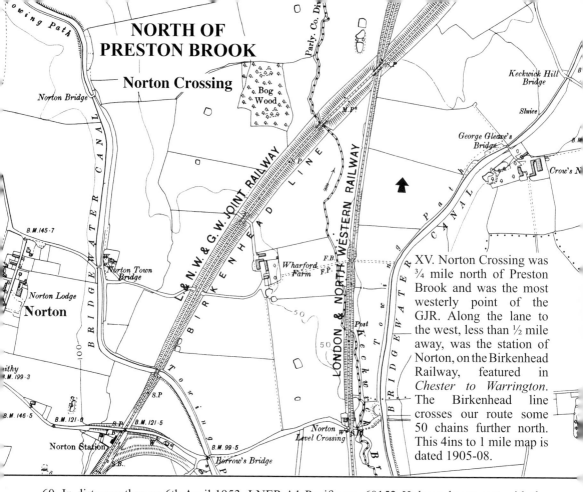

XV. Norton Crossing was ¾ mile north of Preston Brook and was the most westerly point of the GJR. Along the lane to the west, less than ½ mile away, was the station of Norton, on the Birkenhead Railway, featured in *Chester to Warrington*. The Birkenhead line crosses our route some 50 chains further north. This 4ins to 1 mile map is dated 1905-08.

60. In dirty weather on 6th April 1953, LNER A1 Pacific no. 60152 *Holyrood* runs past with the 11.15 Birmingham – Glasgow. Polmadie shed in Glasgow had a couple of these locos around this time to supplement its LMSR express engines. The signal box closed in 1983, following abolition of the road crossing a year earlier. (R.A.Whitfield/RailPhotoprints.uk)

61. On 10th May 1959, no. 46256 *Sir William A. Stanier F.R.S.* heads the up 'Ulster Express'. In the days before mass air travel, this service connected with the Belfast ferry at Heysham and ran thence to London Euston. The signal box is visible above the fourth coach. (R.A.Whitfield/Rail Photoprints.uk)

MOORE

62. An LNWR 'Precedent' class 2-4-0 stands at the up platform with an inspection saloon in about 1905. Note the Saxby and Farmer signal box on the down side. (A.C.Hartless coll.)

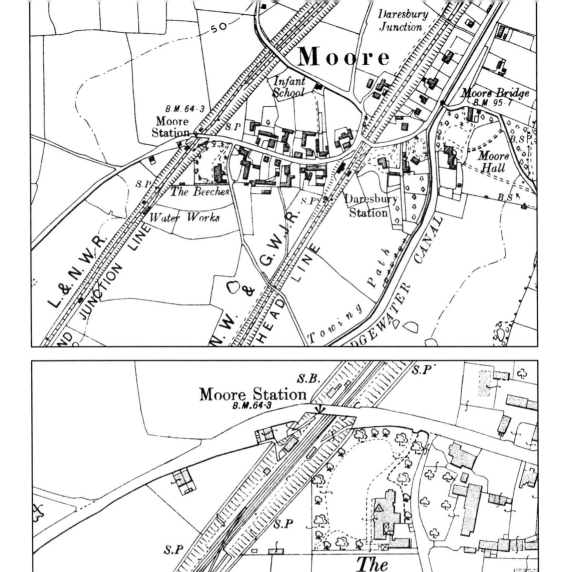

XVI. Moore was some 2¾ miles north of Preston Brook. Here, our route ran in parallel with and west of the Birkenhead Railway. The latter's station, which opened with the line in 1850, was initially also called Moore, but in 1861 it was renamed Daresbury, a village one mile to the south, to avoid confusion. This is featured in the *Chester to Warrington* album. The GJR's approach to Moore is on level track and the LNWR took the opportunity to install water troughs around 500 yards long here. The local water is hard, which is detrimental to locomotive boilers, so a water softening plant, the Water Works on the map, was also constructed. This required a siding for the removal of sludge. The station closed temporarily as a WW2 economy measure from 1st February 1943, but never re-opened, and official closure was confirmed in 1949. There was no goods station. The road spanning the line became the A558 Runcorn to Warrington in 1919, but was subsequently bypassed and downgraded. The top map, scaled at 8ins to 1 mile, is dated 1897; the map beneath it is dated 1910 and scaled at 25ins to 1 mile.

63. Black Five 4-6-0 no. 4862 passes on a down goods in about 1947. At this time, the station was temporarily closed, explaining its neglected appearance. The down side building is the original GJR station of 1837, the sheds on the up side came later. Beyond them is the water softening plant for the troughs to the south of the station. (A.C.Hartless coll.)

64. Two pictures from the evening of 8th July 1967 illustrate the transition from steam to diesel power. Black Five no. 45089 heads northwards across the water troughs with a parcels service. The loco was just a month from withdrawal after 32 years service. (T.Heavyside)

65. English Electric Type 4 no. D315 casts an equally long shadow as it passes with a mixed up freight. The water softening tower catches the light in the background. The troughs were removed soon afterwards with the end of main line steam. (T.Heavyside)

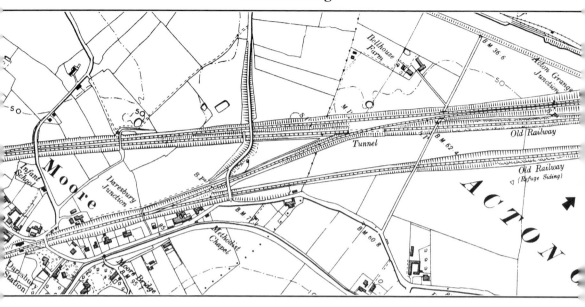

XVII. This 4ins to 1 mile map, dated 1897, is a continuation of the top one on the previous page, with Moore to the left. The GJR and the Birkenhead lines originally ran parallel with one another with a narrow strip of land between, but both were re-aligned when the Manchester Ship Canal, opened in 1894, was constructed. Acton Grange Viaduct was built to carry the four tracks of the two routes across the canal. To gain the necessary clearance over sea-going ships, the previously level GJR line was replaced on its west side by a new alignment climbing at 1 in 135, and joined roughly halfway along the deviation by the Chester line near Bellhouse Farm. Acton Grange Junction precedes the viaduct where there are facing crossovers between the Crewe and Chester lines in both directions.

66. Acton Grange Viaduct signal box straddled the Chester lines, and was in use from 1893 to 1940. (A.C.Hartless coll.)

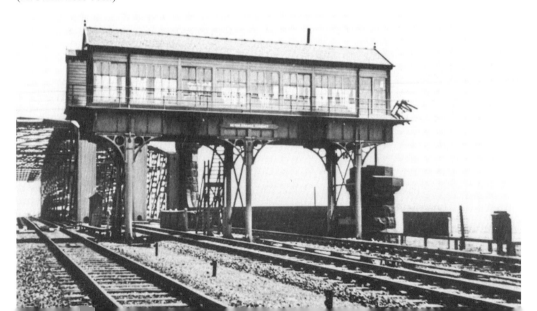

67. On 1st July 1967, 'Britannia' 4-6-2 no. 70046 (no longer carrying its name *Anzac*) runs down the gradient towards Moore with an express freight, probably Carlisle – Crewe, which includes a nuclear fuel flask at the front and grain wagons near the rear. Behind the train is Acton Grange Junction signal box (1940-72), with a signal off for a down train on the Chester line. Beyond that is the superstructure of Acton Grange Viaduct. To the right of the loco, adjacent to an isolated bush, is the old GJR alignment, abandoned in 1893. Above that is the re-aligned Chester route, and beyond that the Bellhouse Lane bridge over its original alignment can be seen. (T.Heavyside)

See also pictures 84-88 in *Chester to Warrington.*

Bank Quay
Soap Works

Iron Works

Engine Shed

Bank Quay
Aluminium
Rolling Mills

Crosfield's High
Level Sidings

Football
Ground

Pavilion

Landing
Stage

Landing
Stages

Landing
Stages

LONDON MIDLAND & SCOTTISH RAILWAY

P & K

Allotment Gardens

S.P.

Sand Pumping
Station

B.M.22·7

Mud

WALTON · INFERIOR

Mud

B.M.23·5

Mud

B.M.24·8

Walton Hey
Farm

Mud

Walton New
Junction

Walton Old
Junction

Baronet Farm

F. House

S.B.

S.P.

S.P.

S.P.

S.P.

M.P.

M.P.

S.P.

F.B.

F.B.

Canoe found
September 189

Runcorn & Latchford Canal (Disused)

Moss Wood

Allotment Gardens Timber Yard

M.P.

M.P.

L.M.S. & G.W. JOINT RAILWAY
BIRKENHEAD LINE

MORLEY
COMMON

Sawing & Planing
Mills

P.

S.P.

MINERAL RAILWAY

MANCHESTER SHIP CANAL

NORTH EAST CHESHIRE RIVERS Catchment Area

Weir

50

B.M.85·8

S.P.

Acton Grange

SOUTH OF WARRINGTON

← XVIII. On its approach to Warrington, the GJR crossed the River Mersey by an elegant two span bridge. Between 1850 and 1893, this was used by both the Crewe and Chester routes, and the connection between them was at Walton Junction, later Walton Old Junction, immediately south of the river. The new alignment to reach Acton Grange Viaduct, graded at 1 in 135, was opened in 1893 to the west of the old one, and at a higher level, including a second Mersey bridge. The low level route was retained to give access to Arpley sidings and the Altrincham line, with a new alignment between Walton Old Junction and Acton Grange Viaduct graded at 1 in 69. Walton New Junction became the point at which the Crewe and Chester routes diverged, until Acton Grange Junction was created ¾ mile further south in 1940. The allotment gardens shown between the two routes south of the Mersey were subsequently replaced by Walton Old Junction Sidings. The sidings at top right comprise Arpley Yard. The line to their right, disappearing at the top right margin, runs to Arpley Junction and connected with the Altrincham line. The Mersey formed the county boundary between Cheshire and Lancashire from time immemorial until the boundary changes of 1974, since when Warrington has been the largest town in the ceremonial county of Cheshire. The town was founded by the Romans, and was the lowest bridging point of the Mersey until the Victorian era. In 1831, the population of the Warrington Poor Law Union district was already 27,757, supporting a variety of industries. In 2011, the population of the unitary borough of Warrington was 202,228. This 1938-39 map is scaled at 6ins to 1 mile.

68. The first Mersey viaduct is illustrated in about 1840, looking west as a train leaves Warrington. To the left is the single span across the Runcorn & Latchford Canal. Altogether there are 12 arches. (A.C.Hartless coll.)

69. In October 1962, 'Jubilee' class no. 45613 *Kenya* is approaching the second Mersey viaduct with a southbound parcels train. From left to right, the three running lines are down slow, down fast and up main. The down slow was subsequently removed. To the right, lower down, is the original route between Warrington and Walton Old Junction with Arpley Sidings beyond. The rear of the train is passing Warrington No. 1 signal box, in use from 1912 to 1972. (J.Carter/RailPhotoprints.uk)

70. On 17th September 1966, 8F 2-8-0 no. 48114 has crossed the second Mersey viaduct with a southbound banana train, possibly from Preston Docks. The bridge is of the same bowstring design as Acton Grange Viaduct. Walton New Junction signal box closed in 1972. (W.A.Brown/J.Suter coll.)

71. On 4th June 1980, no. 87021 *Robert the Bruce* approaches Bank Quay with a down InterCity service. The factory in the background is Thames Board Mills (the parent company was based in Purfleet) which was in business from 1937 to 1983. Arpley Sidings and the low level line to Walton Old Junction occupy the space between the paper mill and the main line. (M.L.Boakes/J.Suter coll.)

72. Walton Old Junction Sidings were visited on 25th June 1991. We are looking south from near the entrance road, which is connected to the low level down line just south of the original Mersey viaduct. The line from Walton Old Junction to Acton Grange can be seen rising in the left background, whilst the main line is on the embankment at right. No. 90045 and a class 47 are in the company of a variety of air-braked wagons in transit; for example, the five on the second road from the left are carrying rock salt from Runcorn and Middlewich to Dalry; on the next road are hoppers carrying lime from Hindlow to Mossend; and on the next two roads are tanks of gas oil from Stanlow to various customers. All of these flows were carried by the Speedlink wagonload freight network which closed in July 1991; the business was not covering its costs in the run-up to privatisation. The overhead electrification was dismantled soon afterwards, but in 2017 the sidings were still used for wagon storage. See also pictures 89-96 in *Chester to Warrington*. (P.D.Shannon)

XIX. When the GJR opened in 1837, Warrington was the only significant town served north of Stafford, 48½ miles away. However, it was not the first passenger carrying railway in the town. That honour befell the Warrington & Newton Railway, which opened a 4¼ mile line from Newton Junction (later Earlestown) on the Liverpool & Manchester Railway on 25th July 1831. Its rudimentary Warrington terminus was at the south end of Dallam Lane, close to Foundry Street.

[continued opposite]

The W&NR also opened a goods branch to Liverpool Road (the continuation of Sankey Street), and the GJR, having acquired the W&NR in 1835 (the first ever takeover of one railway company by another), made an end-on junction with this in 1837 in order to reach the L&MR.

The GJR closed the Dallam Lane station, and located its own, called simply Warrington, north of the Liverpool Road bridge, close to what became Bank Quay Goods Station. The LNWR resited the passenger station to Bank Quay from 16th November 1868 to act as an interchange with the low level line from Widnes to Broadheath (Altrincham) which had come under its control in 1864. The LNWR continued to call the station simply 'Warrington', but the Bank Quay appendage was used increasingly after Warrington Central, on the Cheshire Lines route from Liverpool to Manchester, opened in 1873. Bank Quay is 182 miles from Euston. In 2017, the hourly Euston to Glasgow service made its first call here, with a schedule for most trains of 104 minutes, an average speed of 105mph. This 1938-39 map is scaled at 5ins to 1 mile.

73. On 10th August 1935, LNWR 19" Goods no. 8749 arrives with an Eccles – Llandudno summer Saturday working, passing Crosfield's soap factory (note the trade mark 'PERSIL' half concealed by the loco's chimney). Crosfield's first factory was established in 1814 and by the date of this picture the company was part of the Unilever empire. It was still in production in 2017, under the ownership of PQ Corp, based in the USA. (Bentley coll.)

74. Warrington has been a manufacturing town since the Industrial Revolution, and many of its factories had private sidings. In 1957 there were 51 such rail connections within the borough. In the vicinity of Bank Quay these included Crosfield's and Whitecross Wire Works, north of Liverpool Rd. On 9th July 1954, class 3F 0-6-0T no. 47603 was photographed from the station shunting Crosfield's sidings; the first vehicle is for the conveyance of margarine, which shares many of the same raw materials as soap. (B.Brooksbank)

75. On 4th June 1957, class 8P 4-6-2 no. 46230 *Duchess of Buccleugh* runs through with the 10.05am Glasgow Central – Birmingham New Street. The station layout has barely changed since its construction, comprising two long island platforms including a short north facing bay on the down side. The canopies on both platforms have lost much of their glazing. Behind the loco is Warrington No. 2 signal box, which served from 1925 to 1972, and to its right we see Bank Quay marshalling and carriage sidings. The tail of the train is passing beneath Liverpool Road bridge, beyond which the original station stood from 1837 to 1868. LNWR signals still abound. (R.J.Buckley/Initial Photographics)

76. On 3rd May 1962, class 5MT 4-6-0 no. 73071 is on the down main line with a parcels service. Compared with the previous view, 'Bank Quay' has finally been added to the running-in board, the down platform has been lengthened (note change in style of coping stones), the down side canopy has been replaced by a shorter one, and a lift shaft installed. (G.Coltas/J.Suter coll.)

77. On 1st August 1967, class 9F 2-10-0 no. 92227 is at the up main platform with a lengthy train of empty coaching stock. An English Electric Type 4 diesel is at platform 4, partially concealed by an LMSR general utility van in the down bay. Semaphore signals have been replaced by colour lights, still under the control of No. 2 box. The trio in the right foreground seem to have seen it all before, but main line steam had but a year left. (T.Heavyside)

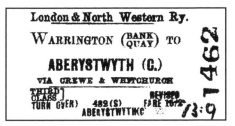

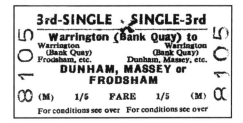

78. On 4th May 1989, no. 47123 is on the up goods loop with a Speedlink service heading for Walton Old Junction sidings. Electrification was effective here from mid-1973. This required the rebuilding of Liverpool Road bridge, and many others. The former marshalling and carriage sidings have been replaced by a car park. (A.C.Hartless)

See also pictures 97-120 in *Chester to Warrington*. **The low level platforms will be featured in a future album.**

---

79. On 20th July 1990, no. 47442 runs down the reversible up slow line with an Arpley – Dallam Freight Terminal trip carrying steel girders and wire coil. The canopy above the up island platform has been renewed, and passengers await the next departure from platform 3. (P.D.Shannon)

NORTH OF WARRINGTON

Dallam

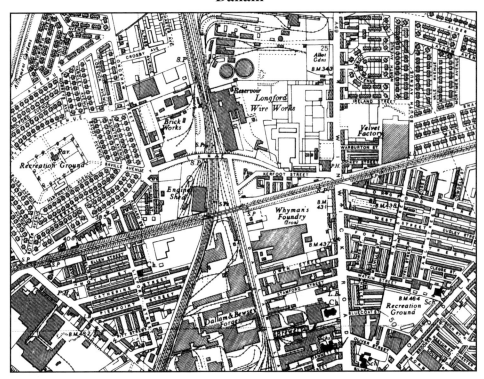

XX. The junction of the Warrington & Newton Railway's lines to Dallam Lane and Liverpool Road is to the left of Longford Wire Works on this 1938 map (4ins to 1 mile). Both lines are bridged by the Liverpool – Manchester route of the Cheshire Lines Committee, this section being the Warrington Central avoiding line. The engine shed was Warrington Dallam, coded 8B by the LMS and BR until closure from 11th August 1968. The last steam workings were on 2nd October 1967. Connections can be seen to the Wire Works on the up side, and to the extensive gas works further north, also to the brick works on the down side. The West Coast Main Line is quadruple track through Warrington, from Acton Grange until Winwick Junction.

80. Dallam motive power depot was built in 1888 as a 10-road straight shed, and is seen here on Sunday 17th July 1955. The locos on view are principally Stanier 5MT 4-6-0s and 8F 2-8-0s, which was often the case right up until the depot closed over 12 years later. Engines shedded here were mostly freight locos. (W.Potter/R.M.Casserley coll.)

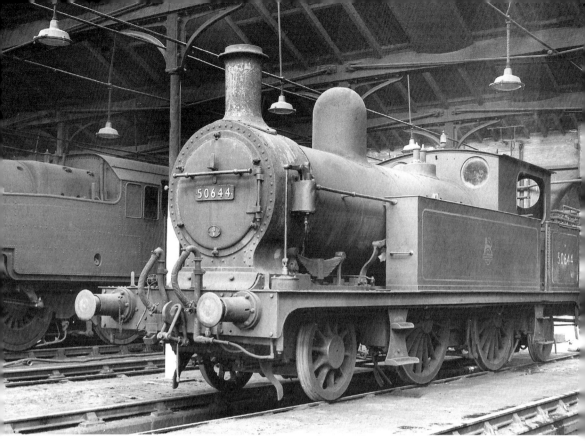

81. Out of traffic at the rear of the shed on 23rd August 1955 was ex-LYR 2-4-2T no. 50644. It spent the last 5½ years of its life allocated here until withdrawal in October 1958. In the background is a class 3MT 2-6-2T. (B.Morrison)

82. The shed was refurbished in 1957 – compare the roof before and after – when one track was removed. On Sunday 2nd October 1960, 5MT 4-6-0 no. 45377, a visitor from Blackpool, is used to draw resident class 3F 0-6-0 no. 43295 from the shed. The main line is out of shot to the left. (H.Ballantyne/Initial Photographics)

83. On 24th August 1966, uncared for class 5MT 4-6-0 no. 73137 rolls a lengthy freight along the up slow line, possibly from Patricroft to Arpley. The line going off the left margin leads to the loco shed; then come the paired down and up through lines. The lines going off the right margin are the remains of the Dallam Branch. All of this was controlled by Dallam Branch Sidings Signal Box on the left. To the right of the loco is Longford Wire Works with the gas works beyond. Dallam Branch Sidings, right background, served both premises. (T.Heavyside)

84. We look in the opposite direction from Folly Lane bridge on 10th April 1990, as no. 08809 shunts Dallam Freight Terminal. Inward consignments of steel in various forms were the main traffic at this time. The alignment of the W&NR's line of 1831 can be inferred from Dallam Lane in the left background; the railway ran alongside it, parallel to the left siding. The up slow of the WCML makes a brief appearance at right. In 2017 the sidings were still in place, but less busy, handling limestone. (P.D.Shannon)

85. Looking north again, on 29th February 2012, no. 66125 shunts wagons of rock salt which will form the 17.00 service to Grangemouth, a trial run that was not repeated. Compare the view with picture 83 to appreciate how the land on either side of the railway has been redeveloped. In the background, above the front of the loco, is Warrington Royal Mail Terminal on the site of the former Dallam Branch Sidings. (P.D.Shannon)

86. Inside Warrington Royal Mail Terminal during an evening in early 2002, we see three examples of class 325 postal EMUs. 16 of these four coach units were built at Derby in 1995 based on the successful dual voltage class 319 passenger version, and painted in Royal Mail red. The terminal opened in 1997 as Royal Mail's main distribution centre for the north west of England. To the left is the long through platform, numbered 1 at the south end and 2 at the north; unit no. 325001 occupies platform 3, and the train at right is in platform 4, both south facing bays. Royal Mail subsequently scaled back its use of rail, but in 2017 Warrington still dealt with four arrivals and four departures a day, being roughly mid-way between similar installations at Willesden (London) and Shieldmuir (Glasgow). (K.Parker)

Winwick Quay

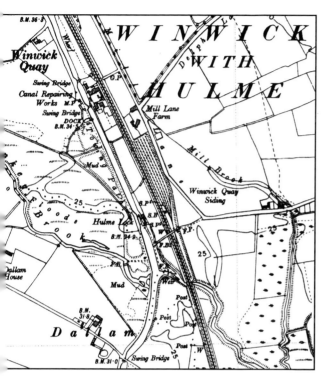

XXI. Winwick Quay was established by the St Helens Canal, which opened in 1757, linking St Helens with the River Mersey at Widnes. It promoted the growth of local industries well before the coming of the railways. The canal eventually fell into disrepair after WW2. Winwick Quay is 2½ miles north of Warrington Bank Quay, and the Warrington & Newton Railway had a stopping place here, which the GJR closed in 1840. This was probably adjacent to the Canal Repairing Works. The LNWR constructed Winwick Quay Sidings as the yards in Warrington became increasingly over-worked. Closure came in the late 1960s. This 1938 map is scaled at 5ins to 1 mile.

87. A northward view of Winwick Quay Sidings on 5th July 1965, seen from the footbridge across the main line. The left hand track is the up slow, separated from the yard by the signal box and a variety of sheds. The locos are 'Jubilee' class 4-6-0 no. 45563 *Australia* with a brakevan, and class 5MT 4-6-0 no. 73125 is shunting. The tower and chimney in the right background are at Winwick Hospital. (RailOnline)

Winwick Hospital

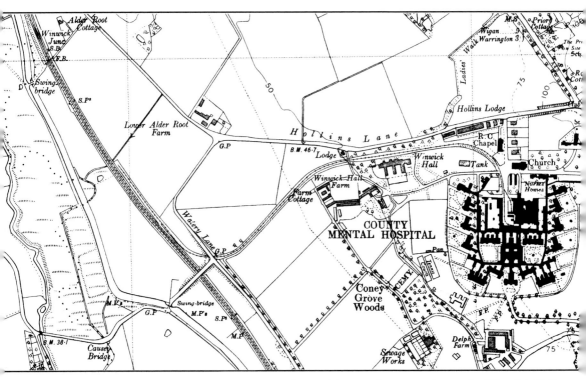

XXII. Half a mile north of Winwick Quay, on the up side, was the connection to the Winwick Hall Mental Hospital. This was a half mile branch which was used to supply coal to power the hospital's boilers. The line closed in about 1960. This map, and the next, were revised in 1947 and are scaled at 4ins to 1 mile. The hospital opened in 1897 and closed 100 years later, in 1997. Most of the buildings were later demolished and replaced by a housing estate.

88. Class 2MT 2-6-2T no. 41212 is propelling a single wagonload of coal towards Winwick Hospital, probably sometime between 1955 and 1958 when the loco was shedded at Dallam. The WCML is to the left. The recently constructed bridge in the middle distance carries Alder Lane, whilst the chimney at right background is at Vulcan Foundry. (G.Drought)

Winwick Junction

XXIII. The Warrington & Newton Railway route of 1831 runs from the bottom of the map to the top left. Running off to the top right is the LNWR's new line, which opened on 1st August 1864 to Golborne Junction. This was built for direct traffic between Warrington and Wigan, and was the last section of the WCML to be opened, avoiding the busy Liverpool & Manchester line and, until 1847, reversal at Parkside. The LNWR quadrupled Warrington to Winwick Jn, from where the two northward routes continued as double track, which was still the arrangement in 2017.

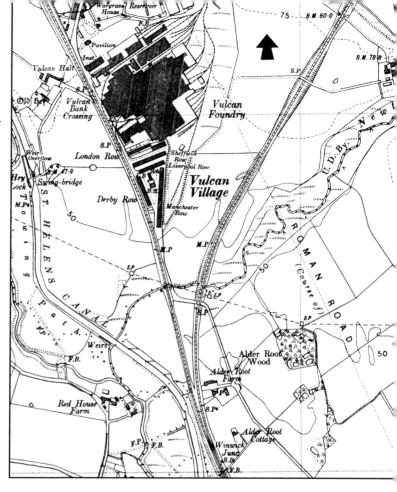

89. This is the classic pre-electrification view of Winwick Junction, seen from the footbridge on 12th February 1961 as no. 46244 *King George VI* comes off the Winwick & Golborne line with the up 'Royal Scot'. The Earlestown line branches off to the left. Vulcan Foundry dominates the background. (H.Ballantyne/Rail Photoprints)

90. Overhead electrification was installed in 1972 on both routes, and control of signalling passed to Warrington Power Signal Box. On 30th May 1990, nos 31120 and 31270 catch the evening sun as they pass with the 17.32 Sellafield – Bridgwater British Nuclear Fuels service, consisting of five nuclear flasks and an assortment of barrier wagons. Vulcan Foundry had become part of Ruston Diesels by this time. Its story, and that of the Winwick Junction to Earlestown line, will be told in a future volume. (P.D.Shannon)

91. In 2017, the latest locomotive type to take to the WCML was the class 88 Vossloh bi-mode Bo-Bo, built in Spain. On 14th June 2017, no. 88003 *Genesis* is seen in electric mode just a few days into its working life at Red Bank, half a mile north of Winwick Junction on the Winwick and Golborne line, with the 06.16 Daventry International Freight Terminal - Mossend, the so-called 'Tesco Express'. (A.Hart)

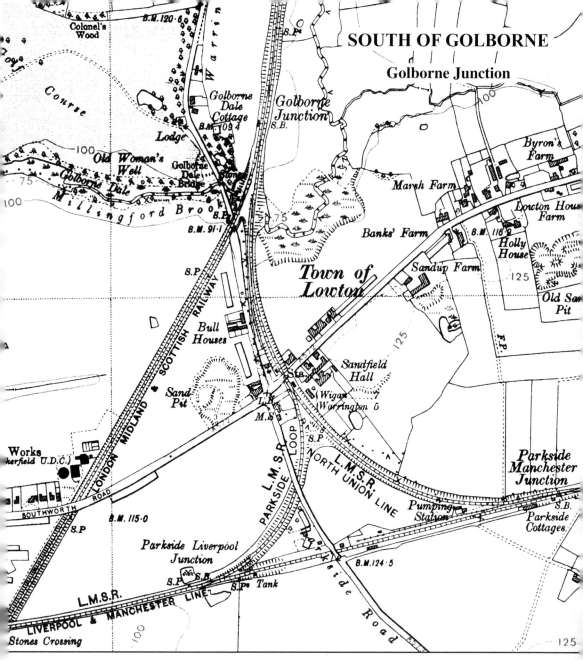

XXIV. The chronology of the railways on this 1938 map (at 8ins to 1 mile) is:
1830: Liverpool – Manchester (left to right across the lower section);
1832: Parkside Manchester Junction – Wigan (Wigan Branch Railway, top of the map);
1847: Parkside Loop (Parkside Liverpool Jn – Lowton Jn);
1864: Winwick Junction (bottom of map) – Golborne Jn.

The Wigan Branch Railway opened on 3rd September 1832. On 22nd May 1834, it was merged with the Wigan & Preston Railway to form the North Union Railway; this was the first ever merger of two railway companies. Golborne Junction is some 2¼ miles north of Winwick Junction. The Winwick and Golborne line is uphill in the down direction with a ruling gradient of 1 in 132 and is mostly in cutting. It passes beneath the Liverpool & Manchester line. Quadruple track resumes at Golborne Junction as far as Wigan.

92. On a day in August 1971, Co-Co no. 433 has just passed Golborne Junction, visible above the rear of the train, with a late afternoon Euston – Blackpool North express made up of Mk I stock. The fast lines are the two furthest from the camera, whilst the nearer slow lines are on the original alignment of the Wigan Branch. The line is still semaphore signalled, but new colour light signals are in the process of installation. The signal box, which closed in September 1972, can be seen in the background, in line with the left hand tower of the two which contained the winding gear of Parkside Colliery. Note also Winwick Hospital on the skyline above the fourth coach. (A.Hart)

93. On 17th July 2017, no. 66429 has just passed Golborne Junction with the 12.46 Carlisle New Yard – Crewe Basford Hall infrastructure service and is running along the two track Winwick and Golborne line. The houses in the background line Golborne Dale Road, the A573, behind which runs the Wigan Branch between Golborne and Lowton Junctions. (A.Hart)

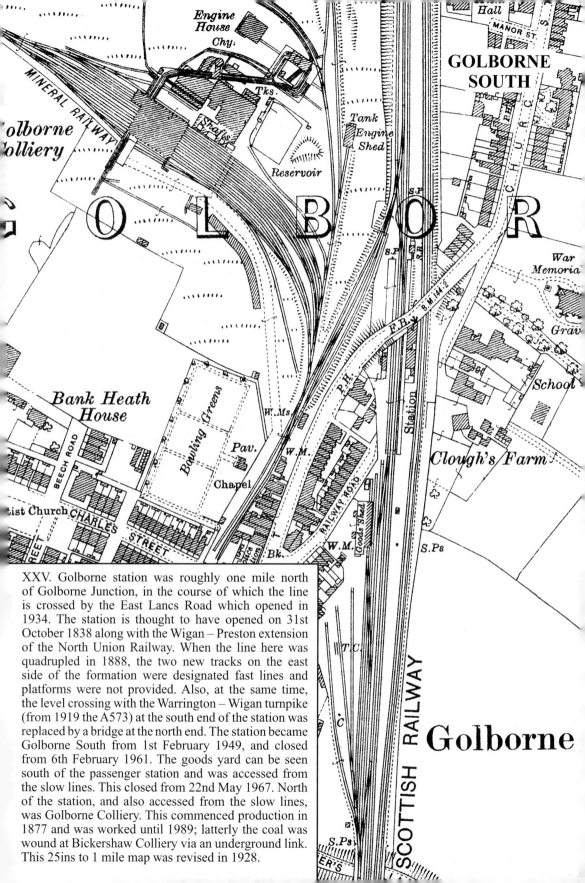

Hall
MANOR ST.

GOLBORNE SOUTH

Engine
House
Chy.

Tks.

Shafts

Tank
Engine
Shed

War
Memoria

Reservoir

Golborne
Colliery

MINERAL RAILWAY

G O L B O R

Grav

School

B M 144·2

P.H.

F.B.

Station

W. Ms

W.M.

Clough's Farm

Bank Heath
House

BEECH ROAD

Bowling Greens

Pav.

Chapel

tist Church CHARLES
STREET

W.M.

RAILWAY ROAD

Bk.

W.M.

Goods Shed

S.Ps

XXV. Golborne station was roughly one mile north of Golborne Junction, in the course of which the line is crossed by the East Lancs Road which opened in 1934. The station is thought to have opened on 31st October 1838 along with the Wigan – Preston extension of the North Union Railway. When the line here was quadrupled in 1888, the two new tracks on the east side of the formation were designated fast lines and platforms were not provided. Also, at the same time, the level crossing with the Warrington – Wigan turnpike (from 1919 the A573) at the south end of the station was replaced by a bridge at the north end. The station became Golborne South from 1st February 1949, and closed from 6th February 1961. The goods yard can be seen south of the passenger station and was accessed from the slow lines. This closed from 22nd May 1967. North of the station, and also accessed from the slow lines, was Golborne Colliery. This commenced production in 1877 and was worked until 1989; latterly the coal was wound at Bickershaw Colliery via an underground link. This 25ins to 1 mile map was revised in 1928.

T.C.

C

SCOTTISH RAILWAY

Golborne

S.Ps

94. Golborne LNWR station was the subject of a postcard, dated around 1910, looking north, taken perhaps from the rear of a goods train or an inspection saloon on the up slow line. The fast lines are out of shot behind the up platform to the right. Between the up slow and the down fast is Golborne No. 2 signal box which closed in 1959. At far left and partially shrouded in smoke is the headstock of Golborne Colliery. (A.C.Hartless coll.)

95. Co-Co no. 430 passes the site of Golborne South with what looks like the same Euston – Blackpool service and stock seen in picture 92 on a different day in August 1971. The position of the former up platform is marked by the waste ground between the two pairs of tracks. Golborne No. 1 signal box can be seen above the rear of the train; this closed in September 1972, when Warrington PSB took control. To the right, the redundant trackwork of the goods station has yet to be removed. (A.Hart)

NORTH OF GOLBORNE

XXVI. Half a mile north of Golborne, on this 1948 map (scaled at 5ins to 1 mile) the line was bridged by the Great Central Railway's St Helens branch of 1895. Its Golborne station became Golborne North on 1st February 1949. The branch closed in 1968 but access was still required to industrial premises at Ashton-in-Makerfield, so a new west to north curve joining the slow lines of the WCML was installed, the connection being known as Haydock Branch Junction. Edge Green Colliery was to the west of the Wigan Branch and much of its output was shipped by the Leigh Branch of the Leeds & Liverpool Canal to the east, which was reached by a railway that passed beneath the main line. The colliery closed in 1928. At this point the main line reaches Golborne Summit at the end of a gentle but almost continuous climb from Warrington.

96. 'Royal Scot' class 7P 4-6-0 no. 46122 *Royal Ulster Rifleman* runs along the down fast with what is most likely a Crewe – Carlisle van train in September 1962. It has just passed beneath the Lowton St. Mary's - St. Helens line, which runs across the background on a long embankment; its Golborne North station was approximately above the fourth vehicle. (J.Carter/Rail Photoprints)

97. In June 1970, English Electric Type 4 no. D302 heads the 19.30 Crewe – Glasgow vans, which includes a MkII coach as the fourth vehicle. The railway bridge has been removed, leaving only the abutments, and the embankment is already less evident. Haydock Branch Junction has been added on the right, giving access to sidings at Ashton-in-Makerfield previously served by the ex-Great Central line. A new warehouse is taking shape in the right background. (A.Hart)

BAMFURLONG

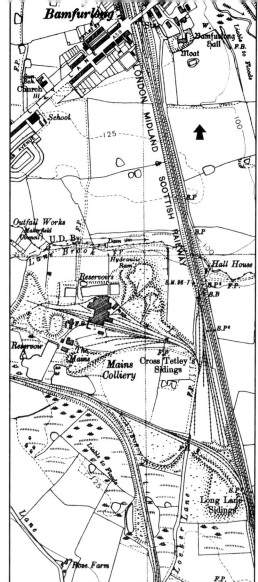

XXVIIa. Bamfurlong was a little over 2 miles north of Golborne. Local pronounciation puts the stress on the first syllable. Coal mining was in progress well before the coming of the railway. Long Lane sidings were the exchange point for Long Lane Colliery, off the left of this map, and which ceased production in the late 1930s. Mains Colliery was a consolidation by Cross Tetley & Co of several smaller pits that were worked from the 1840s. It passed to the Wigan Coal Corporation in the mid 1930s, and closed under NCB ownership in 1960. Bamfurlong station opened on 1st April 1878 and closed on 27th November 1950. There were no goods facilities. As at Golborne, there were platforms only on the slow lines after quadrupling in 1888. This 4ins to 1 mile map was revised in 1938.

98. Like Golborne, Bamfurlong station was not popular with photographers, probably because the expresses passed round the back of the platforms rather than through them. This is a northward view from the 1950s, after closure. The main building appears to be identical to Golborne, with the booking office at street level and steps down to the up platform. The footbridge to the down side is also the same. The shelters here, however, are of timber compared with the more substantial brickwork of Golborne. Another difference is the colliery track behind the down platform. A down express is visible beyond Lily Lane bridge. (A.C.Hartless coll.)

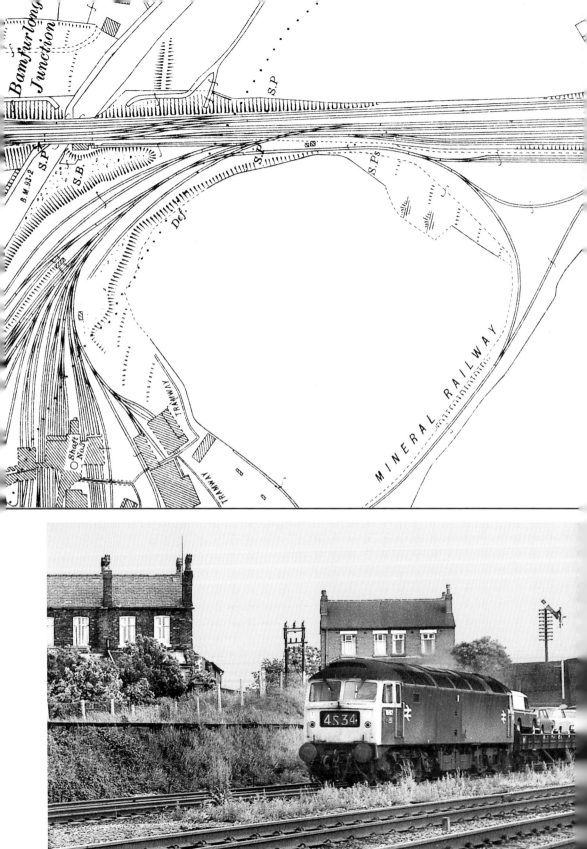

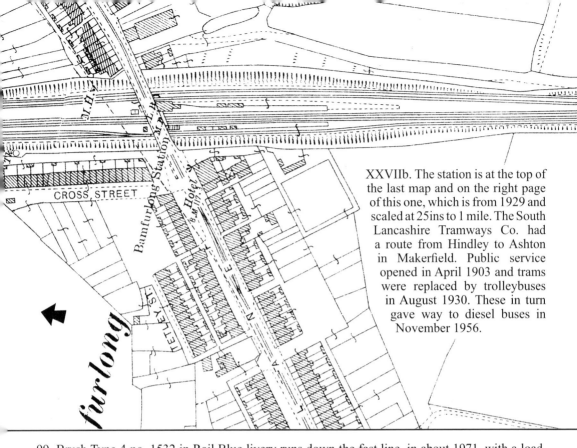

CROSS STREET

Bamfurlong Station

Hotel

TETLEY ST.

CROSS STREET

furlong

XXVIIb. The station is at the top of the last map and on the right page of this one, which is from 1929 and scaled at 25ins to 1 mile. The South Lancashire Tramways Co. had a route from Hindley to Ashton in Makerfield. Public service opened in April 1903 and trams were replaced by trolleybuses in August 1930. These in turn gave way to diesel buses in November 1956.

99. Brush Type 4 no. 1532 in Rail Blue livery runs down the fast line, in about 1971, with a load of new BMC vehicles, probably in transit from Bordesley to Bathgate for distribution in Scotland. The line is still semaphore controlled, although a new gantry in the background shows resignalling is in progress. The site of the station's up platform is visible beyond Lily Lane bridge. The colliery track, which passed beneath the arch on the right, was lifted in the mid 1960s. (A.Hart)

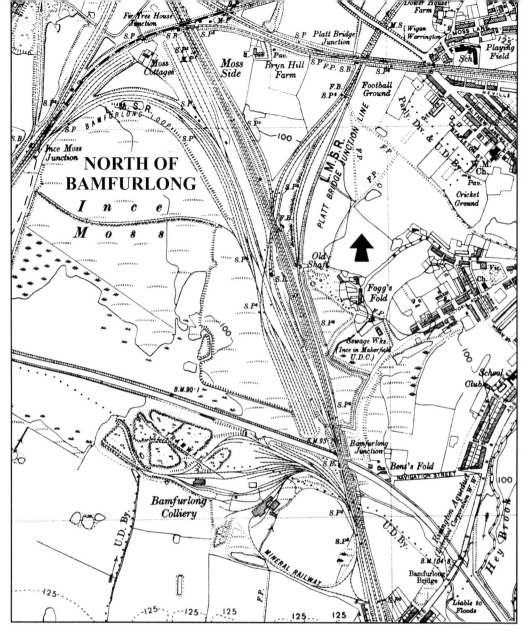

XXVIII. North of the station, on the west side of the line, was Bamfurlong Colliery, as shown on this 1938 map (6ins to 1 mile). This also was owned by Cross Tetley, and was linked to Mains Colliery from 1881 by a single track, which ran alongside the down slow of the main line. The colliery closed in 1936. Next, the line crosses the Leigh Branch of the Leeds & Liverpool Canal. This opened in 1820, only 12 years before the railway; it was still open in 2017.

At Bamfurlong Junction, lines branched both north east and west from the North Union Railway. The north-eastward line was the Platt Bridge Junction of 1889. This was joined directly from the fast lines, but from the slow lines a burrowing junction was required, the tracks passing beneath the main lines to the left of the P of 'PLATT'. Immediately beyond the bridge another pair of tracks, the down and up goods lines, climbed up to run alongside the fast lines, making a six track formation northward to Wigan. The 'SB' just to the south of the bridge was Bamfurlong Sorting Sidings box, immediately south of which was the start of the westward line, the Bamfurlong Loop of 1895 which joined the Wigan – St Helens line. Bamfurlong Sidings were laid out in 1895 to the west of the running lines. [continued opposite]

Those between the canal and Sorting Sidings box were the South End and those to the left of Moss Side were the North End. These were busy yards dealing with local traffic, particularly coal, and longer distance freight alike. The Platt Bridge Junction line was the start of the Wigan Avoiding, or Whelley, Line. This looped around the east of Wigan and rejoined the North Union at Standish Junction, 5¼ miles north of Bamfurlong Junction.

In 2017, all that remained was the four track main line, a single track lead from the down slow at Bamfurlong Junction to Bamfurlong Sidings Junction, which split into the single line Ince Moss Chord (the former Bamfurlong Loop), and the down and up goods lines which still passed beneath the main lines en route to Springs Branch. All lines had been electrified.

100. We have moved some 100 yards north of the previous view, and are again looking back to Lily Lane bridge. On 3rd June 1967, class 5MT 4-6-0 no. 45232 is on the up fast with soda ash wagons, whilst classmate no. 45312 is the Whelley banker awaiting its next duty, and meanwhile displaying the light engine lamp code. Note the pile of ash in front of the loco and the bothy with its leaning chimney. (T.Heavyside)

101. Looking in the opposite direction on the same day, class 8F 2-8-0 no. 48307 is on the up fast with a short freight train. Bamfurlong Junction signal box was a 1961 replacement for an LNWR structure. Beyond it, the lines cross the canal, whilst Bamfurlong Sidings are to the left, obscured by the box. (T.Heavyside)

102. Sometime in the second half of 1962, class 4F 0-6-0 no. 44301 is working a short transfer freight southward along the Springs Branch – Bamfurlong Sidings line and will shortly pass beneath the North Union main lines. Note the ex-WD 2-8-0 and brakevan near Platt Bridge Junction on the Springs Branch – Tyldesley line in the background. (J.Carter/Rail Photoprints)

103. On 18th February 1987, nos 20135 and 20065 are on the down Bamfurlong goods line with empty HAA coal wagons from Fiddlers Ferry, bound for refill at Bickershaw Colliery, which will require a reversal at Springs Branch. The goods lines branch off the slow lines at Bamfurlong Junction, ¾ mile to the south, and pass beneath the main lines before climbing up alongside them. In the right background the north end of Bamfurlong Sorting Sidings is visible; by this date they were used only for storage of redundant wagons and were lifted soon afterwards. (A.C.Hartless)

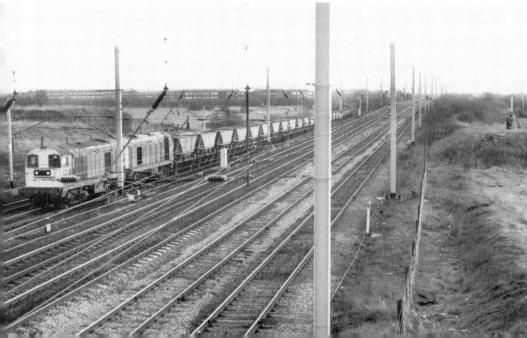

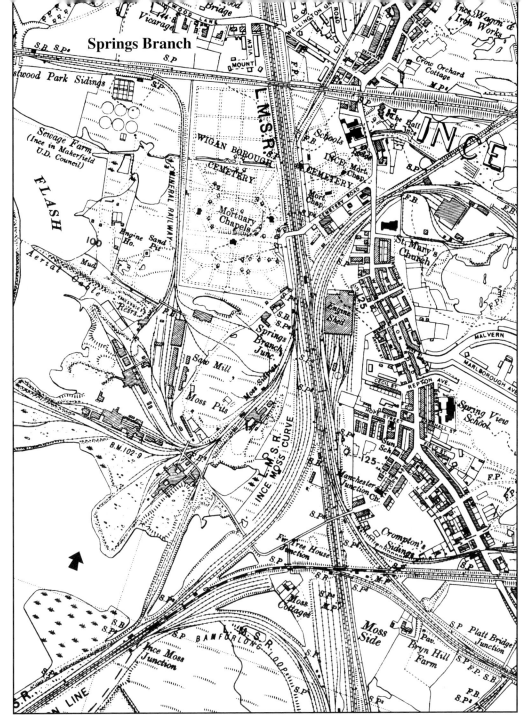

XXIX. Immediately beyond the north end of Bamfurlong Yard, the North Union Railway passed beneath the Lancashire Union Railway at Fir Tree House Junction. The LUR was an LNWR scheme to open a new route between East Lancashire and the Mersey Docks, at Garston, to break the Lancashire & Yorkshire Railway's monopoly on this lucrative traffic. It opened in 1869 and lasted for just a century. The bridge over the six-track NUR lines was demolished in about 1971, prior to electrification. Manchester Junction was where the LNWR's Eccles – Tyldesley – Wigan line of 1864 trailed in. This was a four track route until the passenger service was withdrawn

[continued overleaf]

in 1969, leaving a freight branch serving Bickershaw Colliery until that closed in 1992. In 2017, all that remained was a shunting neck giving access to the former Springs Branch loco shed. Across the main lines from Manchester Junction, the map shows a signal box, which was Springs Branch No. 1. This was built in 1895, there having been earlier smaller versions, and like all the remaining mechanical signalling north of Weaver Junction, its work was transferred to Warrington PSB in 1973, when the main lines were electrified. Behind this box, the Ince Moss Curve trails in. This was opened in 1869 as part of the LUR. It provided a direct link between St Helens and Wigan, and also a shorter route between Liverpool and Wigan than via Parkside. It was electrified in 2015.

The origins of Springs Branch loco shed are obscure, but there is evidence of a rudimentary facility in the 1840s. Thereafter, it was expanded in line with traffic requirements. In 1869, the existing buildings were replaced by a new eight road straight shed, which became No. 1 shed when a second eight road shed, No. 2, was opened alongside in 1882. The map shows two separate fans of track leading to the two halves of the depot. When the LMSR coded its loco depots into districts in 1935, Springs Branch became 10A, the concentration depot for the district covering the former LNWR sheds at Preston, Patricroft, Plodder Lane and Sutton Oak. It was recoded 8F in early 1958, remaining so until it closed to steam from 4th December 1967, just eight months before the total elimination of steam from BR. No. 2 shed was replaced by a diesel depot in 1967, and No. 1 shed was demolished in the mid 1980s. The demise of the coal industry led to the closure of the depot as an operational loco shed, but, in 1997, EWS took it over for the recovery of major components from life expired locomotives, which went on into the mid 2000s. In 2017, the depot was still in use, supporting activities such as permanent way repair, autumnal track spraying and minor loco repairs.

The 'SB' opposite the loco shed was Springs Branch North Sidings, whilst the building between the fast and slow lines close to the north end of the loco shed was Springs Branch No. 2 Signal Box. The first box on this site was installed in 1877, and the final one in 1936. Like No. 1 box, it was de-commissioned in 1973. To the west of the main lines, and with a trailing connection, was Ince Moss Colliery. This was a complex of pits worked over many decades, mostly under the ownership of Pearson & Knowles, and which ceased production in 1960. It was also connected to the Lancashire Union Railway and the Lancashire & Yorkshire Railway.

The Springs Branch itself is the line leaving the North Union behind the engine shed and running to the upper right margin. It dated from 1838 and ran north eastward to serve collieries and other industry in the localities of Ince and New Springs. It never had a passenger service, but was sufficiently busy to be double tracked by the 1850s. The Branch was around 2¾ miles long. The top end of the line closed in the early 1930s, and was further truncated in 1958. The last customer on the Branch, Central Wagon, ceased rail traffic in about 1974. Some of the remaining track was retained for wagon storage, and was eventually lifted in the early 1990s. This 1938 map is scaled at 5ins to 1 mile.

104. A northward view of Shed 10A Springs Branch in 1938 has No.1 shed on the left and No. 2 to the right. The breakdown train occupies number 1 road. (D.K.Jones coll.)

105. This view from 9th August 1953 shows that No. 1 shed has been rebuilt, whilst the roof supports at the front of No. 2 shed have been replaced. Lifting gear has been erected outside No. 1 shed. No. 65199 was a former Great Central Railway 0-6-0, LNER class J10, which was transferred here with other classmates when the ex-GCR shed at Lower Ince was closed the previous year. Class 8F 2-8-0 no. 48733 was a visitor from Bescot. (R.M.Casserley)

106. In October 1962, 'Britannia' 4-6-2 no. 70016 *Ariel* is on the up goods loop with a lengthy train, possibly empty newspaper vans en route to Manchester. It has just passed Springs Branch No. 2 Signal Box. Behind the loco's smokebox is the rear of Springs Branch No. 1 loco shed, whilst the Branch itself swings right, behind the shed. Brewery Sidings contain a variety of wagons and an ex-LYR 0-6-0, which appears to have been dumped. (J.Carter/RailPhotoprints)

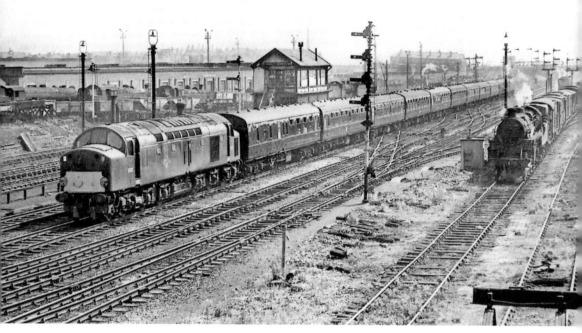

107. In October 1963, English Electric Type 4 no. D302 passes Springs Branch with a down express. Behind the diesel is Springs Branch loco shed, with a line of redundant locos awaiting the call to the scrapyard. Springs Branch No. 2 signal box is prominent. To the right, a Standard class 4MT 2-6-0 is shunting Springs Branch North Sidings. (RailPhotoprints coll.)

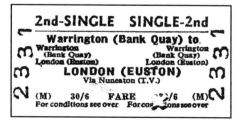

108. No. 2 shed was given a replacement roof in 1955, which can be seen in the right background of this view from 28th June 1965. From left to right the locos are Standard class 4MT 2-6-0 no. 76084 from Lower Darwen, 4F 0-6-0 no. 44350 from Sutton Oak, 4MT 2-6-4T no. 42174, and a grubby 8F 2-8-0. (T.Heavyside)

109. On 29th June 1966, class 5MT 4-6-0 no. 44962 has its tender replenished from the coaling plant. (T.Heavyside)

110. On 16th August 1972, Co-Co no. 444 accelerates away from Wigan with a Euston service. Steam has been vanquished, but there is still much to appreciate in this pre-electrification view. Springs Branch No. 1 Signal Box stands above the locomotive, and behind that runs Ince Moss Curve. The signal cabin above the third coach is Springs Branch North Sidings, above which in the background are the twin chimneys of Westwood Power Station. Springs Branch No. 2 Signal Box is beyond the rear of the train, above which can be seen the two Wigan Gas Works gas holders. Springs Branch No. 1 loco shed has a class 25 and two class 40s in attendance. The taller diesel depot which replaced No. 2 shed is to its right. The former direct line to Manchester Exchange via Tyldesley branches off in the right foreground. (T.Heavyside)

111. On 18th February 1987, no. 86209 *City of Coventry* passes with the 07.30 Aberdeen – Penzance. Westwood Power Station was demolished the following year, but Springs Branch No. 1 loco shed has already been flattened. (A.C.Hartless)

XXX.
(Caption overleaf)

XXX. *[map on previous page]* The last word on the Springs Branch area goes to the Crow Orchard branch. This can be seen running parallel with the up goods line until it turns right alongside Ince Cemetery to terminate at Warrington Road. This site was originally a colliery and was retained as a landsale yard into the mid 1950s. The next landmark on the approach to Wigan was the bridge beneath the LYR's Pemberton Loop, which was in use between 1889 and 1969. The coal fired Westwood Power Station followed with sidings on the down side, although most of its coal was delivered by canal. The line crosses the Leeds & Liverpool Canal at the top margin.

```
┌─────────────────────────────────────────────────────┐
│   2nd - SINGLE          SINGLE - 2nd                  │
│ N                                              N      │
│            Golborne          to                       │
│    Golborne              Golborne              4      │
│    Wigan (N.W.)          Wigan (N.W.)                 │
│   WIGAN (North Western)                        4      │
│  (M)      0/10    FARE   0/10     (M)  O              │
│    For conditions see over  For conditions see over   │
└─────────────────────────────────────────────────────┘
```

112. No. 46229 *Duchess of Hamilton* leaves Wigan with an up express in about 1962. This was the first of the three Coronation Pacifics to be preserved – see front cover and picture 6 for the other two. Like no. 46233, it was purchased by Butlins, and was exhibited at the Minehead Holiday Camp from April 1964 until the end of the 1974 season. After cosmetic restoration, it went on display at the National Railway Museum in May 1976 for two years, after which it was returned to main line working order. It ran from 1980–96 before retiring to the NRM in the condition seen here. Between 2005–09 it was returned to its as-built streamlined condition and was then returned to display at York. At this time there were six tracks between Bamfurlong Junction and here, comprising from left to right, down and up slow, down and up fast, and down and up east loop. In the left background is Wigan No. 1 Signal Box. Otherwise the gas works dominates the scenery with the gas holders behind the train, and the massive retort house to the right. (J.Carter/RailPhotoprints)

113. Looking south from the same point, ex-WD 2-8-0 no. 90183 forges along the down slow with a train of covered hoppers ('covhops'), sometime in 1964. There is yet a seventh running line to the right, the down west loop which extended from the middle distance as far as Wigan station. To the right of this are Canal Bridge, or Westwood, Sidings, which latterly served Westwood Power Station. (J.Carter/RailPhotoprints)

WIGAN NORTH WESTERN

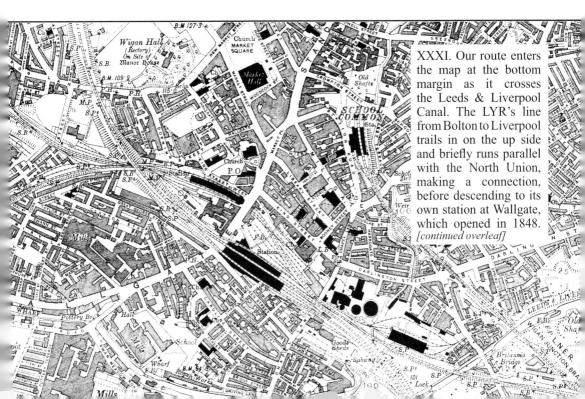

XXXI. Our route enters the map at the bottom margin as it crosses the Leeds & Liverpool Canal. The LYR's line from Bolton to Liverpool trails in on the up side and briefly runs parallel with the North Union, making a connection, before descending to its own station at Wallgate, which opened in 1848. *[continued overleaf]*

Wigan No. 1 Signal Box was in the vee of the NU and LYR lines until closure in 1973; this was an Air Raid Protected (ARP) box of 1942 and replaced three LNWR boxes. On the north side of the Bolton line was the extensive Wigan Gas Works. The compact town centre is evident, with the third station, Wigan Central (1884 – 1964), at School Common. The map is from 1938 and scaled at 4ins to 1 mile.

The terminus of the Wigan Branch Railway was at Chapel Lane. This was in use from 1832–38 until the North Union's extension to Preston opened. Chapel Lane then became the NUR's goods station (the Goods Sheds in the lower middle of the map) and lasted until the demise of wagon load goods traffic in the late 1960s. The new station had its main entrance on Wallgate, which passes from the left of the map, beneath the North Union and above the LYR, to Market Place. The LNWR station became inadequate for late 19th century traffic, and was rebuilt between 1889 – 94. This resulted in five through platforms and five bays, four of them at the south end. It was called simply 'Wigan' until 'North Western' was added in June 1924 after the Grouping.

Following rationalisation in the early 1970s, as part of the electrification of the WCML, the layout in 2017 comprised four through roads and two up bays. The six tracks at Springs Branch merged into four by the Leeds & Liverpool Canal bridge, with the two fast lines flanked by loop lines. North of the station there have only ever been two tracks.

Wigan North Western is 193¾ miles from London Euston. The town obtained its Royal Charter in 1246. The Leeds & Liverpool Canal reached here in 1781 and led to a rapid growth in coal mining. When the Wigan Branch Railway opened in 1832, the town's population was estimated at 21,000. This tripled by the start of the 20th century, mostly as a result of heavy industry, and had further grown to 103,600 by 2011. This map is from 1930 and is scaled at 6ins to 1 mile.

114. On 21st April 1951, this LNWR class 2F 0-6-0 was still carrying its LMSR number, 28580, as it carefully propelled wagons through platform 2. (H.C.Casserley)

115. On 4th June 1957, we see a once commonplace sight of an LNWR 0-8-0, no. 49025 in this case, passing Wigan with a coal train, on the up main. The leading four trucks appear to be new 16 ton BR mineral wagons, which were built by the thousand. Colour light signalling was installed at Wigan at the time the signal boxes were replaced in 1942-43. Note that electric lighting is being installed on platform 3, replacing gas, and also the pigeon basket. The loco obscures south facing bays numbers 1 & 2, and beyond them through platform 1, the up passenger loop. Right of this is Top Yard with an assortment of wagons, crossed by a long footbridge linking the station with King Street. The buildings, beyond that, line Wallgate, one of the town's main thoroughfares. (R.J.Buckley/Initial Photographics)

116. Bays 3 (right) and 4 are seen on 24th April 1965, as 4MT 2-6-4T no. 42456 awaits departure with a southbound local parcels train. A long time resident of Springs Branch, the loco is believed to have been withdrawn at the end of this turn. To its left are through platforms 4 (right) and 5. Note the three dead end roads have no engine release facility. (I.Turnbull/RailPhotoprints)

117. We move to the north end of Wigan North Western on 5th August 1967, as double chimneyed Black Five no. 44766, only days away from withdrawal, calls with a down passenger train, very likely a summer Saturday extra. This was the longest of the five through platforms following the 1894 rebuilding; it was also reversible and had a scissors crossing in the middle so it could deal with two trains simultaneously. To its right is platform 5, the down slow. To its left is bay No. 5, with the main through platforms 2 and 3 beyond. (B.Taylor/J.Suter coll.)

118. The south end is seen sometime in the summer of 1967. Black Five no. 44971 runs into platform 3 with a down extra, possibly going to Blackpool. This loco must have been a good 'un as it survived to the very end of steam in August 1968. The tracks at far left are the former LYR line from Wigan Wallgate to Bolton, which briefly run parallel with the NUR. The gas works is visible beyond the premises on the left, and the flat roof of Wigan No. 1 Signal Box can be seen above the middle of the train. Chapel Street Goods Yard is beyond, and slightly below, the wall at the far right. (T.Heavyside)

119. On 30th July 1982, nos 25315 and 25286 run along the up main with empty oil tanks for Stanlow. The rebuilt station looks bare in comparison with its predecessor; the most obvious difference compared with picture 115 is the removal of the old bay platforms 3 and 4. Mail trollies have not yet been consigned to history, and a class 108 DMU is at platform 2 with a Liverpool service. (T.Heavyside)

120. The south end is seen on 3rd August 1982. No. 47366 is hauling a Merseyrail class 503 EMU to Horwich for overhaul. All six platform faces are in view: number 1 (up passenger loop) is far left beyond the signal, the two bays numbers 2 and 3 are to the right of the signal, number 4 (up main) is left of the locomotive, number 5 (down main) is occupied by the train, and number 6 (down and up passenger loop) is far right. The gas holder, just visible above the loco, is a link with the past. (T.Heavyside)

MP Middleton Press

EVOLVING THE ULTIMATE RAIL ENCYCLOPEDIA

Easebourne Midhurst GU29 9AZ. Tel:01730 813169

www.middletonpress.co.uk email:info@middletonpress.co.uk

A-978 0 906520 B- 978 1 873793 C- 978 1 901706 D-978 1 904474
E - 978 1 906008 F - 978 1 908174 G - 978 1 910356

All titles listed below were in print at time of publication - please check current availability by looking at our website - *www.middletonpress.co.uk* or by requesting a Brochure which includes our *LATEST* RAILWAY TITLES also our TRAMWAY, TROLLEYBUS, MILITARY and COASTAL series

A
Abergavenny to Merthyr C 91 8
Abertillery & Ebbw Vale Lines D 84 5
Aberystwyth to Carmarthen E 90 1
Allhallows - Branch Line to A 62 8
Alton - Branch Lines to A 11 6
Andover to Southampton A 82 6
Ascot - Branch Lines around A 64 2
Ashburton - Branch Line to B 95 4
Ashford - Steam to Eurostar B 67 1
Ashford to Dover A 48 2
Austrian Narrow Gauge D 04 3
Avonmouth - BL around D 42 5
Aylesbury to Rugby D 91 3

B
Baker Street to Uxbridge D 90 6
Bala to Llandudno E 87 1
Banbury to Birmingham D 27 2
Banbury to Cheltenham E 63 5
Bangor to Holyhead F 01 7
Bangor to Portmadoc E 72 7
Barking to Southend C 80 2
Barmouth to Pwllheli E 53 6
Barry - Branch Lines around D 50 0
Bartlow - Branch Lines to F 27 7
Bath Green Park to Bristol C 36 9
Bath to Evercreech Junction A 60 4
Beamish 40 years on rails E94 9
Bedford to Wellingborough D 31 9
Berwick to Drem F 64 2
Berwick to St. Boswells F 75 8
B'ham to Tamworth & Nuneaton F 63 5
Birkenhead to West Kirby F 61 1
Birmingham to Wolverhampton E253
Blackburn to Hellifield F 95 6
Bletchley to Cambridge D 94 4
Bletchley to Rugby E 07 9
Bodmin - Branch Lines around B 83 1
Boston to Lincoln F 80 2
Bournemouth to Evercreech Jn A 46 8
Bournemouth to Weymouth A 57 4
Bradshaw's History F18 5
Bradshaw's Rail Times 1850 F 13 0
Bradshaw's Rail Times 1895 F 11 6
Branch Lines series - see town names
Brecon to Neath D 43 2
Brecon to Newport D 16 6
Brecon to Newtown E 06 2
Brighton to Eastbourne A 16 1
Brighton to Worthing A 03 1
Bristol to Taunton D 03 6
Bromley South to Rochester B 23 7
Bromsgrove to Birmingham D 87 6
Bromsgrove to Gloucester D 73 9
Broxbourne to Cambridge F16 1
Brunel - A railtour D 74 6
Bude - Branch Line to B 29 9
Burnham to Evercreech Jn B 68 0

C
Cambridge to Ely D 55 5
Canterbury - BLs around B 58 9
Cardiff to Dowlais (Cae Harris) E 47 5
Cardiff to Pontypridd E 95 6
Cardiff to Swansea E 42 0
Carlisle to Hawick E 85 7
Carmarthen to Fishguard E 66 6
Caterham & Tattenham Corner B251
Central & Southern Spain NG E 91 8
Chard and Yeovil - BLs a C 30 7
Charing Cross to Dartford A 75 8
Charing Cross to Orpington A 96 3
Cheddar - Branch Line to B 90 9
Cheltenham to Andover C 43 7
Cheltenham to Redditch D 81 4
Chester to Birkenhead F 21 5
Chester to Manchester F 51 2
Chester to Rhyl E 93 2
Chester to Warrington F 40 6
Chichester to Portsmouth A 14 7
Clacton and Walton - BLs to F 04 8
Clapham Jn to Beckenham Jn B 36 7
Cleobury Mortimer - BLs a E 18 5
Clevedon & Portishead - BLs to D180
Consett to South Shields E 57 4
Cornwall Narrow Gauge D 56 2
Corris and Vale of Rheidol E 65 9
Coventry to Leicester G 00 5
Craven Arms to Llandeilo E 35 2
Craven Arms to Wellington E 33 8
Crawley to Littlehampton A 34 5
Crewe to Manchester F 57 4
Crewe to Wigan G 12 8
Cromer - Branch Lines around C 26 0
Croydon to East Grinstead B 48 0
Crystal Palace & Catford Loop B 87 1
Cyprus Narrow Gauge E 13 0

D
Darjeeling Revisited F 09 3
Darlington Leamside Newcastle E 28 4
Darlington to Newcastle D 98 2
Dartford to Sittingbourne B 34 3
Denbigh - Branch Lines around F 32 1
Derby to Chesterfield G 11 1
Derby to Stoke-on-Trent F 93 2
Derwent Valley - BL to the D 06 7
Devon Narrow Gauge E 09 3
Didcot to Banbury D 02 9
Didcot to Swindon C 84 0
Didcot to Winchester C 13 0
Dorset & Somerset NG D 76 0
Douglas - Laxey - Ramsey E 75 8
Douglas to Peel C 88 8
Douglas to Port Erin C 55 0
Douglas to Ramsey D 39 5
Dover to Ramsgate A 78 9
Drem to Edinburgh G 06 7
Dublin Northwards in 1950s E 31 4
Dunstable - Branch Lines to E 27 7

E
Ealing to Slough C 42 0
Eastbourne to Hastings A 27 7
East Cornwall Mineral Railways D 22 7
East Croydon to Three Bridges A 53 6
Eastern Spain Narrow Gauge E 56 7
East Grinstead - BLs to A 07 9
East Kent Light Railway A 61 1
East London - Branch Lines of C 44 4
East London Line B 80 0
East of Norwich - Branch Lines E 69 7
Effingham Junction - BLs a A 74 1
Ely to Norwich C 90 1
Enfield Town & Palace Gates D 32 6
Epsom to Horsham A 30 7
Eritrean Narrow Gauge E 38 3
Euston to Harrow & Wealdstone C 89 5
Exeter to Barnstaple B 15 2
Exeter to Newton Abbot C 49 9
Exeter to Tavistock B 69 5
Exmouth - Branch Lines to B 00 8

F
Fairford - Branch Line to A 52 9
Falmouth, Helston & St. Ives C 74 1
Fareham to Salisbury A 67 3
Faversham to Dover B 05 3
Felixstowe & Aldeburgh - BL to D 20 3
Fenchurch Street to Barking C 20 8
Festiniog - 50 yrs of enterprise C 83 3
Festiniog 1946-55 E 01 7
Festiniog in the Fifties B 68 8
Festiniog in the Sixties B 91 6
Ffestiniog in Colour 1955-82 F 25 3
Finsbury Park to Alexandra Pal C 02 8
French Metre Gauge Survivors F 88 8
Frome to Bristol B 77 0

G
Galashiels to Edinburgh F 52 9
Gloucester to Bristol D 35 7
Gloucester to Cardiff D 66 1
Gosport - Branch Lines around A 36 9
Greece Narrow Gauge D 72 2

H
Hampshire Narrow Gauge D 36 4
Harrow to Watford D 14 2
Harwich & Hadleigh - BLs to F 02 4
Harz Revisited F 62 8
Hastings to Ashford A 37 6
Hawick to Galashiels F 36 9
Hawkhurst - Branch Line to A 66 6
Hayling - Branch Line to A 12 3
Hay-on-Wye - BL around D 92 0
Haywards Heath to Seaford A 28 4
Hemel Hempstead - BLs to D 88 3
Henley, Windsor & Marlow - BLa C77 2
Hereford to Newport D 54 8
Hertford & Hatfield - BLs a E 58 1
Hertford Loop E 71 0
Hexham to Carlisle D 75 3
Hexham to Hawick F 08 6
Hitchin to Peterborough D 07 4
Holborn Viaduct to Lewisham A 81 9
Horsham - Branch Lines to A 02 4
Huntingdon - Branch Line to A 93 2

I
Ilford to Shenfield C 97 0
Ilfracombe - Branch Line to B 21 3
Industrial Rlys of the South East A 09 3
Ipswich to Diss F 81 9
Ipswich to Saxmundham C 41 3
Isle of Man Railway Journey F 94 9
Isle of Wight Lines - 50 yrs C 12 3
Italy Narrow Gauge F 17 8

K
Kent Narrow Gauge C 45 1
Kettering to Nottingham F 82-6
Kidderminster to Shrewsbury E 10 9
Kingsbridge - Branch Line to C 98 7
Kings Cross to Potters Bar E 62 8
King's Lynn to Hunstanton F 58 1
Kingston & Hounslow Loops A 83 3
Kingswear - Branch Line to C 17 8

L
Lambourn - Branch Line to C 70 3
Launceston & Princetown - BLs C 19 2
Leek - Branch Line From G 01 2
Leicester to Burton F 85 7
Lewisham to Dartford A 92 5
Lincoln to Cleethorpes F 56 7
Lincoln to Doncaster G 03 6
Lines around Stamford F 98 7
Lines around Wimbledon B 75 6
Liverpool Street to Chingford D 01 2
Liverpool Street to Ilford C 34 5
Llandeilo to Swansea E 46 8
London Bridge to Addiscombe B 20 6
London Bridge to East Croydon A 58 1
Longmoor - Branch Lines to A 41 3
Looe - Branch Line to C 22 2
Loughborough to Nottingham F 68 0
Lowestoft - BLs around E 40 6
Ludlow to Hereford E 14 7
Lydney - Branch Lines around E 26 0
Lyme Regis - Branch Line to A 45 1
Lynton - Branch Line to B 04 6

M
Machynlleth to Barmouth E 54 3
Maesteg and Tondu Lines E 06 2
Majorca & Corsica Narrow Gauge F 41 3
March - Branch Lines around B 09 1
Market Drayton - BLs around F 67 3
Market Harborough to Newark F 86 4
Marylebone to Rickmansworth D 49 4
Melton Constable to Yarmouth Bch E031
Midhurst - Branch Lines of E 78 9
Midhurst - Branch Lines to F 00 0
Minehead - Branch Line to A 80 2
Mitcham Junction Lines B 01 5
Monmouth - Branch Lines to E 20 8
Monmouthshire Eastern Valleys D 71 5
Moretonhampstead - BL to C 27 7
Moreton-in-Marsh to Worcester D 26 5
Morpeth to Bellingham F 87 1
Mountain Ash to Neath D 80 7

N
Newark to Doncaster F 78 9
Newbury to Westbury C 66 6
Newcastle to Hexham D 69 2
Newport (IOW) - Branch Lines to A 26 0
Newquay - Branch Lines to C 71 0
Newton Abbot to Plymouth C 60 4
Newtown to Aberystwyth E 41 3
Northampton to Peterborough F 92 5
North East German NG D 44 9
Northern Alpine Narrow Gauge F 37 6
Northern France Narrow Gauge C 75 8
Northern Spain Narrow Gauge E 83 3
North London Line B 94 7
North of Birmingham F 55 0
North of Grimsby - Branch Lines G 09 8
North Woolwich - BLs around C 65 9
Nottingham to Boston F 70 3
Nottingham to Lincoln F 43 7
Nuneaton to Loughborough G 08 1

O
Ongar - Branch Line to E 05 5
Orpington to Tonbridge B 03 9
Oswestry - Branch Lines around E 60 4
Oswestry to Whitchurch E 81 9
Oxford to Bletchley D 57 9
Oxford to Moreton-in-Marsh D 15 9

P
Paddington to Ealing C 37 6
Paddington to Princes Risborough C819
Padstow - Branch Line to B 54 1
Pembroke and Cardigan - BLs to F 29 1
Peterborough to Kings Lynn E 32 1
Peterborough to Lincoln F 89 5
Peterborough to Newark F 72 7
Plymouth - BLs around B 98 5
Plymouth to St. Austell C 63 5
Pontypool to Mountain Ash D 65 4
Pontypridd to Merthyr F 14 7
Pontypridd to Port Talbot E 86 4
Porthmadog 1954-94 - BLa B 31 2
Portmadoc 1923-46 - BLa B 13 8
Portsmouth to Southampton A 31 4
Portugal Narrow Gauge E 67 3
Potters Bar to Cambridge D 70 8
Princes Risborough - BL to D 05 0
Princes Risborough to Banbury C 85 7

R
Railways to Victory C 16 1
Reading to Basingstoke B 27 5
Reading to Didcot C 79 6
Reading to Guildford A 47 5
Redhill to Ashford A 73 4
Return to Blaenau 1970-82 C 64 2
Rhyl to Bangor F 15 4
Rhymney & New Tredegar Lines E 48 2
Rickmansworth to Aylesbury D 61 6
Romania & Bulgaria NG E 23 9
Romneyrail C 32 1
Ross-on-Wye - BLs around E 30 7
Ruabon to Barmouth E 84 0
Rugby to Birmingham E 37 6
Rugby to Loughborough F 12 3
Rugby to Stafford F 07 9
Rugeley to Stoke-on-Trent F 90 1
Ryde to Ventnor A 19 2

S
Salisbury to Westbury B 39 8
Sardinia and Sicily Narrow Gauge F 50 5
Saxmundham to Yarmouth C 69 7
Saxony & Baltic Germany Revisited F 71 0
Saxony Narrow Gauge D 47 0
Seaton & Sidmouth - BLs to A 95 6
Selsey - Branch Line to A 04 8
Sheerness - Branch Line to B 16 2
Shenfield to Ipswich E 96 3
Shrewsbury - Branch Line to A 86 4
Shrewsbury to Chester E 70 3
Shrewsbury to Crewe F 48 2
Shrewsbury to Ludlow E 21 5
Shrewsbury to Newtown E 29 1
Sierra Leone Narrow Gauge D 28 9
Sirhowy Valley Line E 12 3
Sittingbourne to Ramsgate A 90 1
Skegness & Mablethorpe - BL to F 84 0
Slough to Newbury C 56 7
South African Two-foot gauge E 51 2
Southampton to Bournemouth A 42 0
Southend & Southminster BLs E 76 5
Southern Alpine Narrow Gauge F 22 2
Southern France Narrow Gauge C 47 5
South London Line B 46 6
South Lynn to Norwich City F 03 1
Southwold - Branch Line to A 15 4
Spalding - Branch Lines around E 52 9
Spalding to Grimsby F 65 9 6
Stafford to Chester F 34 5
Stafford to Wellington F 59 8
St Albans to Bedford D 08 1
St. Austell to Penzance C 67 3
St. Boswell to Berwick F 44 4
Steaming Through Isle of Wight A 5
Steaming Through West Hants A 6
Stourbridge to Wolverhampton E 1
St. Pancras to Barking D 68 5
St. Pancras to Folkestone E 88 8
St. Pancras to St. Albans C 78 9
Stratford to Cheshunt F 53 6
Stratford-u-Avon to Birmingham D
Stratford-u-Avon to Cheltenham C
Sudbury - Branch Lines to F 19 2
Surrey Narrow Gauge C 87 1
Sussex Narrow Gauge C 68 0
Swaffham - Branch Lines around F
Swanage to 1999 - BL to A 33 8
Swanley to Ashford B 45 9
Swansea - Branch Lines around F
Swansea to Carmarthen E 59 8
Swindon to Bristol C 96 3
Swindon to Gloucester D 46 3
Swindon to Newport D 30 2
Swiss Narrow Gauge C 94 9

T
Talyllyn 60 E 98 7
Tamworth to Derby F 76 5
Taunton to Barnstaple B 60 2
Taunton to Exeter C 82 6
Taunton to Minehead F 39 0
Tavistock to Plymouth B 88 6
Tenterden - Branch Line to A 21 5
Three Bridges to Brighton A 35 2
Tilbury Loop C 86 4
Tiverton - BLs around C 62 8
Tivetshall to Beccles D 41 8
Tonbridge to Hastings A 44 4
Torrington - Branch Lines to B 37
Tourist Railways of France G 04 3
Towcester - BLs around E 39 0
Tunbridge Wells BLs A 32 1

U
Upwell - Branch Line to B 64 0
Uttoxeter to Macclesfield G 05 0

V
Victoria to Bromley South A 98 7
Victoria to East Croydon A 40 6
Vivarais Revisited E 08 6

W
Walsall Routes F 45 1
Wantage - Branch Line to D 25 8
Wareham to Swanage 50 yrs D 0
Waterloo to Windsor A 54 3
Waterloo to Woking A 38 3
Watford to Leighton Buzzard D 4
Wellingborough to Leicester F 73
Welshpool to Llanfair E 49 9
Wenford Bridge to Fowey C 09 3
Westbury to Bath B 55 8
Westbury to Taunton C 76 5
West Cornwall Mineral Rlys D 48
West Croydon to Epsom B 08 4
West German Narrow Gauge D 9
West London - BLs of C 50 5
West London Line B 84 8
West Wiltshire - BLs of D 12 8
Weymouth - BLs A 65 9
Willesden Jn to Richmond B 71
Wimbledon to Beckenham C 58
Wimbledon to Epsom D 62 6
Wimborne - BLs around A 97 0
Wirksworth - Branch Lines to G
Wisbech - BLs around C 01 7
Witham & Kelvedon - BLs a E 8
Woking to Alton A 59 8
Woking to Portsmouth A 25 3
Woking to Southampton A 55 0
Wolverhampton to Shrewsbury
Wolverhampton to Stafford F 79
Worcester to Birmingham D 97
Worcester to Hereford D 38 8
Worthing to Chichester A 06 2
Wrexham to New Brighton F 47
Wroxham - BLs around F 31 4

Y
Yeovil - 50 yrs change C 38 3
Yeovil to Dorchester A 76 5
Yeovil to Exeter A 91 8
York to Scarborough F 23 9